Sharing Your Faith with People of Other Faiths

David C. Cooper

SHARING YOUR FAITH WITH PEOPLE OF OTHER FAITHS

Printed in the United States of America.

For information, contact Dr. David C. Cooper, 2055 Mount Paran Rd. NW, Atlanta, Georgia 30327.

CONTENTS

INTRODUCTION

CHAPTER ONE
THE MAIN BUSINESS   7

CHAPTER TWO
THE INVASION OF ISLAM   27

CHAPTER THREE
WHAT'S NEW ABOUT NEW AGE?   43

CHAPTER FOUR
JUDAISM AND JESUS   57

CHAPTER FIVE
IS THE EAST REALLY ENLIGHTENED?   87

CHAPTER SIX
WAR IN THE HEAVENLIES   103

*To my congregation
at Mount Paran Central
Church of God.*

INTRODUCTION

When I resigned my first pastorate after 10 years of fruitful ministry, the first person I led to Christ in that church gave me a letter-opener as a going away gift. It bore the inscription:

Thank you for giving to the Lord.
I am a life that was changed.

Without question, the greatest experience in any Christian's life is leading someone to know Jesus Christ as Savior and Lord.

But how do we do that? The very thought of personal witnessing terrifies many. We fear rejection. Or, we're not sure we can answer every question someone might raise about the Bible.

Also, the influx of other religious orientations into American life has changed the face of evangelism.

This book was written to help believers understand some of the religions and philosophies gaining ground in

America today. Such understanding enables us to witness intelligently and confidently about our faith.

The key to sharing one's faith is to keep the focus on Jesus. As one Hindu said, "There is no one seriously bidding for the heart of the world except Jesus Christ."

It is my prayer that this book will inspire you to *"go and tell what great things the Lord has done for you"* (Mark 5:19).

Dr. David C. Cooper

1

The Main Business

Then Jesus said to them, "Do not be afraid.
Go and tell my brothers to go to Galilee;
There they will see me."
Matthew 28:10

 N OLD GERMAN ADAGE SAYS, "The main business is to keep the main business the main business." What then is the main business of the church? In a word the main business is evangelism.

Each of the Gospel writers exercised care in closing out their writings with the final commission of Christ to His church. Matthew recorded Him saying, "Go, therefore, and make disciples of all nations" (Matt 28:19). Mark noted, "Go into all the world and preach the gospel to every creature" (Mk 16:15). Luke recorded, "You shall be witnesses...to the ends of the earth" (Acts 1:8). John portrayed Christ on the resurrection morning declaring to a huddled group of terrified disciples, "Peace be with you! As the Father has sent me, I am sending you" (Jn 20:21).

How is the modern church faring in this business of evangelism? Researcher George Barna interviewed a number of pastors and asked them how Christ would rate their churches if He returned today. Less than half of one percent said He would rate them highly effective. Forty-three percent said He would find them respectable. Only 53 percent said He would rate them as having little positive impact on souls or society. In his book *Evangelism That Works*, Barna notes that only one out of every three Christian churches offers evangelistic training for their people.

Chuck Colson, in his book *The Body*, points out that the modern church in America has lost the focus of its mission.

He issues a solemn challenge:

So, while the church may seem to be experiencing a season of growth and prosperity, it is failing to move people to commitment and sacrifice. The hard truth is that we have substituted an institutionalized religion for the life-changing dynamic of a living faith...When compared with previous generations of believers, we seem among the most thoroughly at peace with our culture, the least adept at transforming society and the most desperate for a meaningful faith. Our *raison d'etre* is confused, our mission obscured, and our existence as a people in jeopardy.[1]

If evangelism is so important, what is it? The word *evangelism* means the announcement of good news—the good news of God in Jesus Christ. Evangelism is not the announcement of an idea, a system, or a principle but a rather a Person. Hence, Mark's Gospel begins with the statement, "The beginning of the gospel about Jesus Christ, the Son of God" (Mk 1:1).

Rather than being coerced, forced, or manipulated, evangelism springs naturally from the believer's heart that overflows with the love of God for the world (Rom 5:5). Evangelism can be defined as the outflow of the inner life. Jesus said, "Out of (your) innermost

That's evangelism— "a lot of Jesus sticks out of us."

being shall flow rivers of living water" (Jn 7:38). And, "Out of the abundance of the heart the mouth speaks" (Matt 12:34). E. Stanley Jones once said that the Holy Spirit is like electricity—He never goes in where He can't come out!

A little boy came home from Sunday School a bit troubled and said to his mother, "Mommy, my Sunday School teacher told me today if I invite Jesus into my heart that he would come in there and live in me." His mother replied, "That's right, sweetheart, he will." With a look of concern on his face he said, "But Mom, won't a lot of him stick out?" That's evangelism. A lot of Jesus sticks out of us.

Evangelism does not consist of a department within the church operated by a handful of gifted, qualified specialists. Rather, evangelism runs throughout and links together every facet of the church's ministry providing unity of purpose. All specialized ministries within the church are designed to fulfill the commission to evangelize the world. While certain evangelists do serve in full-time ministry (Eph 4:12) and pastors are instructed to "do the work of an evangelist" (2 Tim 4:5), evangelism remains the work of the people of God.

The active words in Christ's commission are the words *go* and *tell*. On the resurrection morning Jesus told the women who saw Him first, "Go and tell" (Matt 28:10). The commission raises several important questions: What does telling involve? What are we to tell? How can we best tell the message?

Telling The Message

Jesus commissioned the Church to *go* and *tell*. Last year I spoke with a minister who was leaving his pastorate to assume the call to full-time evangelism. He said to me, "The Lord told me to go, so I am going. My church is well. The pastorate is a joy. But the Lord is telling me to go." I responded by saying that the Lord is always saying *go*.

Seldom, if ever, does He say *stay*. It would be interesting, I added, to study the Scriptures for references to God telling His people to *stay* versus telling them to *go*.

In reality Christ commands His church to *go*. Life with Christ is an adventure of ever-unfolding possibilities, challenges and opportunities. After Pentecost the early church stayed in Jerusalem although they had been commissioned to go into all the world. As far as they were concerned, "all the world" meant their own private world— their own comfort zone.

There they stayed—enjoying the fellowship, teaching and personal ministry. The people met together daily for worship and celebration (Acts 2:42; 5:12). Prayers were answered. Healings occurred. Luke tells us what a glorious atmosphere prevailed among them: "All the believers were one in heart and mind. No one claimed that any of his possessions was his own, but they shared everything they had" (Acts 4:32). The church exploded with growth, "praising God and enjoying the favor of all the people. And the Lord added to their number daily those who were being saved" (Acts 2:47).

However, something was missing. The longer they stayed the more ingrown they became. Congregational contention and administrative hassles began to emerge (Acts 6). All along the Holy Spirit was nudging them to *go*. But they were content to *stay*.

Then something unusual happened. One of the deacons named Stephen was arrested by a delegation of the Sanhedrin for preaching Christ. Confronted by the high priest to answer charges of blasphemy, he delivered one of the most prophetic sermons recorded in the New Testament (Acts 7). The punch line was anything but acceptable to his hearers: "You stiff-necked people, with uncircumcised hearts and ears! You are just like your fathers: You always resist the Holy Spirit!"

The incident resulted in the tragic stoning of Stephen. In the midst of tragedy, however, faith triumphed. "Look," he said, "I see heaven open and the Son of Man standing at the right hand of God." As the last stone struck his body, he slumped to the ground and whispered his final prayer, "Lord, do not hold this sin against them."

What Satan meant for evil, God used for good. Luke tells us that "On that day a great persecution broke out against the church at Jerusalem, and all except the apostles were scattered throughout Judea and Samaria" (Acts 8:1). Persecution became an instrument in the hand of the Holy Spirit to *scatter* the church. No longer would they be content to *stay*. From now on they would *go*.

As we go, we are to tell.

In the same way that God scattered these early believers, He desires to scatter us throughout the world as we "go and tell." Peter calls believers, "God's elect, strangers in the world, scattered throughout (the world)" (1 Pt 1:1, parenthesis added). The word *strangers* means "those placed alongside of," indicating that God strategically places believers beside unbelievers who carefully observe their lives and witness. The word *scattered* (*diaspora*, Greek) refers to scattering seed, giving us a word picture of God scattering His people throughout the world as a farmer scatters seed for harvest.

As we go, we are to tell. The word *tell* (*appangello*, Greek) means to announce, to declare, or to report. Throughout the New Testament 11 different Greek words are translated *tell*. Telling the gospel involves a two-fold process: preaching and teaching, or evangelism and discipleship. According to Matthew, Jesus "went throughout Galilee, *teaching* in their synagogues, *preaching* the good news of the kingdom, and healing every disease and sickness among the people" (Matt 4:23).

Philips Brooks defined preaching as "truth through personality." The New Testament writers place emphasis on both the act of preaching and the content of the message preached. Several key words emerge: (1) *euangelizo* meaning to herald the good news (Luke 4:18,19); (2) *kerruso* meaning to herald, to proclaim, and to publish (2 Tim 4:2); (3) *kerugma* meaning a message or proclamation, stressing the substance or content of what is preached (1 Cor 2:4; 2 Tim 4:17); (4) *logos* meaning a word, denoting the substance of the message (1 Cor 1:18); and (5) *didasko* meaning to teach, train, and give instruction (Matt 4:23; John 14:26).

Telling involves every aspect of communicating the gospel of Christ in word and deed to win converts and develop them into dedicated disciples. We see these dual ministries of preaching and teaching in the ministry of Ezra.

After the Babylonian exile, Ezra occupied a key role in rebuilding the Jerusalem temple and restoring the city. As part of the restoration, the Feast of Tabernacles was celebrated during which Ezra read the Law and proclaimed God's word.

The biblical account reads like a commentary on a pentecostal revival meeting:

Ezra praised the Lord, the great God; and all the people lifted their hands and responded, 'Amen! Amen!' Then they bowed down and worshipped the Lord with their faces to the ground (Neh 8:6).

The Levites followed Ezra's dynamic preaching with in-depth teaching of the Scripture:

The Levites...instructed the people in the Law while the people were standing there. They read from the Book of the Law of God, *making it clear* and *giving the meaning* so that the people could understand what was being said (Neh 8:7,8; emphasis added).

WHAT ARE WE TO TELL? ────────────────

The question is raised, What is our message? Today, there exists a growing sense of confusion among church leaders as to what message to proclaim. Several years ago I read the following heart-penetrating statement in an editorial in *Fortune* magazine: "What we of the world need is a word from the Lord. We look to the church for that word and all we hear is the echo of our own voices."

We know that we are to proclaim the gospel of Christ, but what does that mean? In the New Testament the gospel is described as:

- the gospel of *God* because it originates in the heart of God rather than the mind of man (Rom 1:1);
- the gospel of *Christ* for it sets forth the person and work of Christ (Rom 1:16);
- the gospel of *His Son* emphasizing Christ's deity (Rom 1:9);
- the gospel of *peace* which reconciles God and man (Eph 6:15);
- *my* gospel (Rom 16:15) and *our* gospel (2 Cor 4:3) because we personalize it;
- the gospel of *great joy* resulting from God's salvation (Lk 2:10);
- the gospel of the *kingdom* stressing the dominion of Christ (Matt 24:14);

- the *eternal* gospel since salvation is provided for all people in all ages (Rev 14:6);
- the gospel of *grace* revealing the unmerited favor of God (Acts 20:24); and
- the gospel of your *salvation* underscoring the goal of the gospel—to seek and to save those who are lost (Eph 1:13).

Paul warns us against being misled by a "different gospel" (Gal 1:6). In our day of pluralism—the blending of pagan religions, philosophies and theologies—we are called upon to set ourselves for the defense of the gospel.

Sitting in a Roman prison Paul wrote to the Philippians, "I am put here for the defense of the gospel" (Phil 1:16). The word *defense* (*apologia*) means a verbal defense, a speech, or an answer founded on reason and experience. Peter tells us, "Always be prepared to give an answer to everyone who asks you to give the reason for the hope that you have" (1 Pt 3:15). The word *reason* (*logon*) means a sound, logical and rational explanation for one's faith.

Defending the gospel involves disarming prejudices and overcoming objections to the truth. In reality, five objections to the truth of Christ need to be confronted by the church today:

- all religions lead to God;
- truth is relative;
- man is the measure of all things;

- morality is situational; and
- eternity is a myth.

These objections require confrontation by the church in order for evangelism to flourish.

Since our task is to tell the world what Jesus told the world, we need to explore anew His message. Here is a summary of His message. Jesus preached:

- the kingdom of God (Matt 4:17);
- forgiveness of sins in Himself (Matt 9:2);
- abundant life in all aspects (Matt 6:33; Jn 10:10);
- the necessity of repentance and faith in Him for salvation (Lk 13:3; 24:47);
- freedom from guilt and shame (Jn 8:11);
- the call to discipleship (Lk 9:23; 14:26,27,33);
- a new standard of life (Matt 5-7);
- the promise of eternal life for believers and the certainty of eternal judgment for the wicked (Jn 5:29; Lk 16:19-31);
- the necessity of the new birth for salvation (Jn 3:3,5,7);
- the love of God for the world demonstrated in His sacrificial death and triumphant resurrection (Jn 3:16);
- His second coming to consummate the kingdom (Matt 24:1-35; Mk 13:1-37; Lk 17:20-37); and
- God's concern for every area of human need (Lk 12:32; Matt 14:14).

Perhaps Luke best summed up the preaching of Jesus. One Sabbath, while worshipping at the Nazareth synagogue, Jesus stood before the people and read from the scroll of Isaiah:

> The Spirit of the Lord is on me, because he has anointed me to preach good news to the poor. He has sent me to proclaim freedom for the prisoners and recovery of sight to the blind, to release the oppressed, to proclaim the year of the Lord's favor (Lk 4:18-19).

Both the church collectively and believers individually go every day into the marketplace with the confidence that says, "The Spirit of the Lord is on me, because he has anointed me to preach good news!"

SHARPENING OUR SKILLS

As noted earlier only one out of every three Christian churches offers personal witness training. Many believers feel inadequate, anxious, or even guilt-ridden when the subject of personal witnessing is mentioned. So, what makes an effective witness?

Passion
When Jesus saw the crowds, "He had compassion on them, because they were harassed and helpless, like sheep

without a shepherd" (Matt 9:36). Paul said, "Christ's love compels us" (2 Cor 5:14).

We sense Paul's deep passion for the lost in his letter to the Romans:

> I have great sorrow and unceasing anguish in my heart. For I could wish that I myself were cursed and cut off from Christ for the sake of my brothers...my heart's desire and prayer to God for the Israelites is that they may be saved (Rom 9:2, 3a; 10:1).

Notice the connection between the words *desire* and *prayer*. Passion for the lost comes from prayer. In prayer the Holy Spirit breaks our hearts and fills us with the burden of the Lord. Genesis 6:6 tells us that God's "heart was filled with pain" as He saw the lostness of humanity prior to the flood. Is His heart any less painful today?

The question comes: Do we really believe people are lost? Do we still believe in a place called hell, *sheol* or *hades*—a place Jesus described as one of eternal punishment (Matt 25:46), outer darkness (Matt 8:12; 22:13; 25:30), unquenchable fire (Mk 9:43,44), weeping and gnashing of teeth (Matt 13:42,50), everlasting fire (Matt 25:41,46), perpetual memory ("their worm does not die," Isa 66:24; Mk 9:46-48), and eternal sin (Mk 3:29)?

Have we forgotten Jesus' account of a rich man who died and in "hell, where he was in torment, saw Abraham far away?" He begged for a drop of water to cool his tongue, and petitioned Abraham to send the poor man Lazarus back to his five brothers to "*warn* them so that they will not also come to this place of torment" (Lk 16:19-31).

Do we believe that in the end of all things, when the final chapter of human history is written, that the Revelator's words will be fulfilled? "Then death and hell were thrown into the lake of fire. If anyone's name was not found written in the book of life, he was thrown into the lake of fire" (Rev 20:14,15).

> *Do we really believe people are lost?*

I do not claim to know or understand everything about hell. The very thought of hell makes me tremble. However, in the words of Mark Twain, "It's not what I don't understand about the Bible that troubles me; it's what I do understand that troubles me."

Whatever constitutes hell, I am convinced that hell means eternal separation from God and from all that is holy, good and blessed. To lose sight of this sobering reality quenches the evangelistic fire of the Spirit in the Church and dooms us to ministerial mediocrity. Maybe this explains why 50 to 60 churches close their doors permanently every week in America. The great missionary C. T. Studd said, "Some people want to live within the sound of a church bell. I'd rather run a rescue shop within a yard of hell."

Jesus came to "seek and to save what was lost" (Lk 19:10). Paul testified that He came into "the world to save sinners—of whom I am the worst" (1 Tim 1:15). For this same purpose—to seek and to save those who are lost—we too are sent.

Exposure

Evangelism begins with exposure to the gospel of Christ. Blind Bartamaeus knew to call on Jesus to heal him because, at some point, he had heard about Jesus (Mk 10:47). He had been exposed to the good news.

Faith in Christ begins with hearing, whether it be by sermon, radio, television, Christian music, drama, literature, or personal testimony. Paul reminds us that "faith comes from hearing the message, and the message is heard through the word of Christ" (Rom 10:17).

The largest crowd Charles Spurgeon ever addressed came the night he spoke in the Crystal Palace to a crowd of 23,654 people. A mutiny had occurred in India protesting Britain's rule over that land, and a service of national humiliation was planned. Spurgeon was selected to deliver the sermon.

The night before the service he went to the Crystal Palace to test the acoustics since the building was not constructed with religious services in mind. As he stood on the platform he repeated the verse, "Behold the Lamb of God which takes away the sin of the world." His words were heard by a man working somewhere in the building. The man came to Spurgeon several days later to say that those words had touched his heart. That night alone in the Crystal Palace he received Jesus Christ.

Friendship

Jesus was called the "friend of sinners" (Matt 11:19). His friendship bore the marks of eating and drinking with sinners. He related to people on a social level. This provided the context for His evangelism.

At Jacob's well He struck up a casual conversation with a dejected woman which eventually lead not only to her salvation but the evangelism of an entire village (Jn 4). The point is this—if I desire to witness, I too must be a friend of sinners.

The magnetism of Jesus was His unconditional love for all people. He accepted people as they were—no strings attached. As a result they felt worthwhile, valuable, and important to God. The need to love and to be loved is the deepest need within us all.

Recently, a young woman walked into my office for a counseling appointment. As she began to share her story of pain and guilt, she paused and said to me, "The reason I came to see you is because I knew you would not judge me." The fruit of the Spirit is love. People are drawn to the healing power of Christ's love within us when we become friends of sinners.

No wonder William Barclay challenged us by saying, "The Christian dare not say, 'I care not what men say or think of me.' He must care—for his life is a testimony for or against his faith." Martin Luther reminded us, "Every man is called to be Christ to his neighbor."

In A.D. 252 a deadly plague broke out in the city of Carthage. Cyprian, the Christian bishop of the city, gathered his congregation together. They buried the dead and nursed the sick after the pagans had thrown out the bodies of their dead and fled the city for terror. The church saved the city at the risk of their own lives. This is what the command means, "Love your neighbor as yourself."

Dialogue

People today are no longer conditioned to accept information at face value. The breakdown of authority at all levels of society, as well as the influence of relativism in regard to moral and spiritual truth, has bred into us a sense of skepticism. We want proof!

To address the need for dialogue, a Socratic method of evangelism is proposed by many today, stressing the importance of believers being well-versed in their beliefs so as to be able to effectively pose and answer questions regarding the faith. Dialogue provides a context for the convicting work

We want proof!

of the Spirit who reveals Jesus Christ to human hearts (see Jn 16:7-11).

Open discussion demonstrates respect for other's viewpoints and seeks to build relationships. People today resist the impersonal approaches (door-to-door, television, street witnessing) while being more open to a relational approach—the touchstone for current evangelism.

Persistence

In reality evangelism constitutes spiritual warfare. Therefore, we must "stand and having done all, stand" (Eph 6:13). Winning converts requires persistence in our witness, ministry and intercession.

George Muller, prince of intercessors, spent his life praying for five friends. After five years one of his friends accepted Christ. After 10 years two more were saved. After 25 years a fourth was converted. He continued praying for his fifth friend until he himself died. The man received Christ a few months after Muller's death. Muller had prayed for that man for over 50 years.

Are we tired of praying? Witnessing? Preaching? Ministering? "Let us not become weary in doing good, for at the proper time we will reap a harvest if we do not give up" (Gal 6:9).

Focusing Our Efforts

Where should we focus our efforts? Researcher George Barna encourages the church to redirect its evangelistic focus to reach *young people*. The American church spends 80 percent of its efforts to reach adults when research clearly shows that two-thirds of all Christians accept Christ *before* age 18.

In his research of America's most effective churches Barna found that, without exception, each placed strong emphasis on youth ministry and, in fact, spent 5 to 10 times the money on evangelism (primarily to reach youth) than the average congregation.

Barna also noted other characteristics of effective churches which underscore the importance of evangelism:

- an evangelistic culture fostered by the pastor;
- a ministry philosophy with evangelism at its core;
- frequent and strategic evangelistic events, including weekend services;
- a pastor who spends one to two hours per week planning evangelistic outreach;
- a congregation that is networked to non-Christians;
- cooperation with other churches in the community;
- "stealing" the best ideas that have worked for other churches;
- programs that are innovative, risk-taking and aggressive; and
- effective evangelism training. [2]

May our prayer be that prayer of Jim Elliot, who gave his life carrying the gospel of Christ to the Auca Indians.

Lord, make me a crisis man.
Not just a signpost on the highway of life,
but a fork in the road;
so that men who meet me
will come to know Jesus Christ!

2

THE INVASION OF ISLAM

HE WORD *ISLAM* SIMPLY MEANS submission or peace, denoting submission to the will of God. A young camel driver named Ubu'l-Kassim, later known as Muhammad ("one highly praised") pioneered the religion of Islam. He was born in A.D. 570 in the city of Mecca located in Arabia. Followers of Islam became known as Muslims which means "those who submit to God."

Even though Muhammad was born into the leading tribe of Mecca, the *Koerish,* he knew the meaning of suffering. Both his parents died before he was six. As a young man he began working with caravans and at 25 went to work for a wealthy widow named Khadija as the manager of her caravan business. They eventually married although she was 15 years his senior. It is interesting to note that some of her relatives were Christian. In fact her uncle was bishop of the Nestorian church.

Muhammad spent considerable time in spiritual contemplation. He observed the lawlessness and wars among the Arabian tribes. He also questioned the validity of the Arabian animistic religion which worshipped some 360 false gods around a black stone called the *Kaaba*. Among these deities were angels, demons, and a chief god called *Al-eela* (the god).

Muhammad often prayed and meditated alone in a cave at Mount Hira, outside Mecca. He became engrossed with the name *Al-eela*, one of the Arabic deities in the Kaaba who had no image (later the name was changed to *Allah* meaning God.) When he was 40 years old he entered the cave at Hira where he claimed to have been confronted by the angel Gabriel. While meditating on the name Allah, he heard the angel's voice in the cave commanding him to proclaim. Three times the voice said, "Proclaim!" After the third time Muhammad asked, "What shall I proclaim?" The answer came:

Three times the voice said, "Proclaim!"

Cry - in the name of thy Lord!

Who created man from a blood clot.
Cry! Thy Lord is wondrous kind
Who by thy pen has taught mankind
Things they knew not (being blind).

THE KORAN

The experience terrified him, believing it to be demonic. Muhammad often suffered periodic seizures resulting in trance-like states which he questioned as being either demonic or divine. His wife encouraged him in his metaphysical experiences and became his first convert. She told him that he would become a great prophet.

During periodic visits to the Hira cave he received additional revelations, the contents of which constitute much of the Koran. For the next 22 years he propagated his new religion. During this time he memorized all 78,000 words (114 chapters) of the Koran and transmitted his teachings orally. Today Islam is reported to be the fastest growing religion in the world.

HISTORICAL DEVELOPMENTS

The Cultural Conflict

At first few people accepted Muhammad's simple message which emphasized sharing their wealth with the poor to gain assurance of the afterlife and focused on a Day of Judgment with severe punishment for the unbeliever. However, his denouncement of idol worship threatened the livelihood of businessmen in Mecca. As a result, followers of Muhammad were often beaten or stoned.

In A.D. 622 his own life was threatened. He fled Mecca and went to Yathrib 250 miles away. The flight is known as the *Hegira*, which marks the beginning of the Muslim era. Also, Yathrib was renamed *Medina*, meaning the city of the prophet.

The Conquest of Mecca

He assembled a fighting force and developed the concept of *jihad*, the holy war, which promises immediate entrance into Paradise for those who die in battle. He ruled as a king and a prophet during this time after the *Hegira* (flight) as he built his following.

In 628, Muhammad led 10,000 troops toward Mecca and conquered the city. Within only 10 years after his *Hegira* he controlled all of Arabia. In 632, four years after conquering Mecca, he died in the arms of his favorite wife Aisha whom he married when she was only seven years old.

The Prophetic Succession

Aku Bakr succeeded Muhammad and established the system of religious leaders known as *caliphs*. His succession of Muhammad was marked by violent acts and murders as he exercised his newly inherited power.

Muslim armies bent on conquest spread the Islam belief to India, across North Africa, and into Spain. The famous Battle of Tours (732) prevented Islam from conquering all of Europe. An Islamic capital was established in Baghdad which headed a regime spreading over three continents.

Cultural Influences

The Islamic Empire lasted for 1,000 years. Arabs developed the concept of algebra, designed the architectural pointed arch seen even in Europe's great cathedrals, and introduced such produce as sugar, paper, apricots and rice to the West. Constantinople (modern day Istanbul, Turkey) became the capital of the Ottoman Empire which lasted until 20th century (World War I.)

RELIGIOUS DISTINCTIVES

The Prophets

The seven Great Prophets of Islam include: Adam, Abraham, Moses, David, Solomon, Jesus and Muhammad (the last and greatest prophet possessing the full revelation of Allah). However, only Jesus is referred to as sinless in the Koran. Even Muhammad had to repent of his sins.

The Koran mentions 25 prophets and Islam recognizes over 100,000 prophets, all supposedly carrying the same message. Other caliphs or successors have followed in Muhammad's steps.

The Koran (the sacred book of Islam)

According to Muslim belief Islam was the first religion which God revealed in three books: the Torah, the Psalms (Zabur) and the book of Jesus (Injeel, Evangel). However, man corrupted these books so God sent the angel Gabriel to Muhammad with a new book, the Koran (*Qur'an*).

The Koran consists of three sections: (a) Old Testament excerpts, (b) New Testament excerpts, and (c) Muhammad's revelations which came to him over twenty years consisting of 114 *surahs* or chapters. Muslims believe every word of the Koran was dictated by God. The Koran, then, is the only infallible word of God which is believed to have existed from eternity in a preserved tablet. The teachings of the Koran are supplemented by the traditions of the *Hadith*.

> *"There is no God but Allah and Muhammad is his prophet."*
> — *Islam*

Islam regards the Bible as a corrupt rule of faith inferior to Muhammad's message. However, the Koran reveals a blending of various religious influences including Arabian ceremonies and fasting regulations, Zoroastrian (Persian and Indian) beliefs, and strong elements of Judaism and Christianity. Muhammad learned the religion of the Jews and Christians from at least two sources. First, Jews and Christians lived in his hometown of Mecca. Second, he encountered Jews and Christians through his travels with caravan trade.

The Five Pillars of Islam

Confession. The Islamic creed (*Shahada*) states, "There is no God but Allah, and Muhammad is his prophet." Devout Muslims repeat the creed five times a day.

Prayer. Prayer is offered five times a day (morning, noon, late afternoon, sunset and before bedtime). It usually reciting includes the first chapter of Koran which takes about three minutes to pray. Muslims gather for prayer in mosques at noon on every Friday, the holy day of the week. Sermons are also delivered during the service. Muslims wash their feet, arms and hands, as well as discard their shoes before entering the mosque. The posture for prayer is always kneeling, facing eastward toward Mecca. Originally they faced toward Jerusalem (although Muhammad never actually visited Jerusalem), but when the Jews rejected him as a prophet, he changed the direction to Mecca.

A portion of the opening *surah* of the Koran reads:

> *Praise belongs to God, Lord of the Worlds,*
> *The Compassionate, the Merciful,*
> *King of the day of Judgment.*
> *'Tis thee we worship and thee we ask for help.*
> *Guide us in the straight path.*
> *The path of those whom thou hast favored,*
> *Not the path of those who incur thine anger*
> *not of those who go astray.*
> *He is not begotten nor does he beget.*

Fasting. During Ramadan fasting lasts from sunrise to sunset. Eating and drinking occurs from the evening to the early morning hours. Ramadan is the holy month celebrating Muhammad's initial commission and the revelation of the Koran, and also his famous flight (*Hegira*) from Mecca to Medina. Fasting signifies self-discipline and submission to Allah.

Pilgrimage (Hajj). Each Muslim makes a pilgrimage to Mecca at least once during his lifetime to insure his salvation. While there he walks around the *kabba* (a building which houses a sacred black stone supposedly from Eden), which Gabriel carried to earth. The *kabba* is said to have been originally built by Abraham and Ishmael at the place where Abraham first prayed to God.

Almsgiving. Muslims are required to give two-tenths of one percent of their income in Muslim countries to the poor. Also, freewill offerings (*sadaqah*) are given to the mosques.

Important Teachings and Practices

No God but Allah. Allah is unknowable. As a result, Muslims cannot experience a personal relationship with God. He is transcendent (above and beyond us) not imminent (present with us). Islam discounts the doctrine of the Trinity as presented in both the Old and New Testaments. Allah has 99 known names represented on a rosary (worry beads); only the camel knows the 100th name.

The supremacy of Muhammad in the succession of prophets. Muhammad is honored as the greatest of all prophets.

Everything in life is predestined by Allah. One must be content with his lot in life and be grateful. Every event of life expresses Allah's will.

Salvation is based on good works. The only way to absolutely guarantee entrance into Paradise is to be martyred. Hence, as he was dying, Muhammad claimed that he had been poisoned by the Jews. The concept of heaven involves Muslims receiving everything they were denied in this life. There is a river of liquor, and Muslim men are surrounded by celestial maidens (the *houriyat*) and prepubescent girls (*qasiraat*). Eternal judgment in hell awaits those whose evil deeds outweigh the good.

Missionary activity focuses on territories not individual conversions. A nation is considered Muslim if those in political power are Muslim regardless of whether or not the people are Muslim. Its missionary work aims to establish the kingdom of God over territories and countries bringing the social, political and economic institutions under the rule of Allah. Missionary activity does not focus on personal conversions. A deliberate strategy among some Muslims involves Muslim men marrying Christian women in non-Muslim countries then moving them back to their country, making the household Muslim. Any children born into the household are automatically Muslim.

The ministry of angels. One of the ways Allah reveals His will is through angels. The four archangels include: (1) *Gabriel* who revealed the Koran, (2) *Michael* who supplies man's needs, (3) *Asrafel* who will blow his trumpet to announced the Day of Judgment, and (4) *Asrael* who examines men's souls at the Resurrection. Also included among the angels is Satan who was expelled from Eden because he refused to obey Adam and Allah.

Two classes of people. Those who have submitted to Allah (*Dar ul-Islam*) and those who resist (*Dar ul-harb*). Those who resist are objects of missionary activity, financial pressure and holy war (*jihad*).

The person and work of Jesus Christ. The Koran honors Jesus as a great prophet and even validates His virgin birth. However, Muslims do not understand who the Holy Spirit is who breathed upon Mary as recorded in the Koran. His crucifixion is discounted because they cannot fathom God allowing His prophet to be treated so cruelly. Muslims believe Jesus was translated to heaven before the crucifixion and will return to earth in the last days to judge the world.

> *The Koran honors Jesus as a great prophet.*

The role of women. Women possess limited rights and status in orthodox Islam. Wives live in total submission to the will of their husbands. In the case of divorce the husband exercises complete rights over the children. Muhammad himself had 13 wives. The Koran teaches that it is customary for a man to have only four wives at a time but he must treat each one with equal respect and care. Women keep their heads covered, their faces veiled, and wear the ankle-length *chador* in strict Muslim countries. While women are permitted to make the pilgrimage to Mecca, they are not allowed to enter the *Kabba*.

Various practices include: mandatory circumcision; services for the dead; forbidding music and statues in mosques; permitting polygamy; abstaining from alcohol, drugs, pork and gambling; sounding the *minarets* which call the people to prayer; the law of apostasy which allows for persecution of other faiths, especially Jews and Christians; strict laws and severe punishment for lawbreakers as outlined in the code of ethics known as the *Shari'a* (the path to follow). Even usury is forbidden in the code forcing some Mideastern banks to devise creative ways for charging interest.

The goal of Islam. To bring the entire world in subjection to Allah and his laws by force or persuasion. However, not all Muslims support such extreme and aggressive efforts. Many practice Islam as a way of tolerance and brotherhood.

Jews and Christians. The Koran breathes hot and cold concerning Jews and Christians. Extreme Muslim fanatics decry the abomination of both while moderate Muslims accept Jews and Christians, who are called "the people of the Book." The Koran states twice that "Jews and Christians and whoever believes in God...and does what is right shall have nothing to fear or regret." [3] Other passages encourage Muslims to fight Jews and Christians.

The Major Sects of Islam

The *Wahhabi*, originating in the 18th century, require strict obedience to the Koran as seen in Saudi Arabia's moralistic rule.

The *Shiites* (meaning *partisans*) claim to be direct descendants of Muhammad and heirs to his spiritual leadership. While Muhammad had no sons who survived him, his cousin Ali who married his daughter Fatima, is regarded by the Shiites as the prophetic successor. Shiites represent about a tenth of the Muslim world. The late Ayatollah Khomeini of Iran represents this sect.

The *Sunnis* (from "the tradition of the Prophet") represent 90 percent of Muslims who nominate their leaders in each community since Muhammad left no directives about prophetic succession. Islam, like most religions, represents a fragmented faith consisting of diverse sects which, by the way, remains one of its strengths.

Two other offshoots need mentioning:
Sufism, which constitutes a small group of Muslims,

stresses the desire to know Allah personally through mystical union and experiences. The founder, Melvana Rumi, developed the school for the famous "whirling dervishes," a drug-induced dance art designed to bring the dancers (exclusively young boys) into a mystical trance. Rumi's facilities can still be visited in Konya, Turkey.

The *Black Muslim* movement began in 1913 by a North Carolina man named Timothy Drew, who moved to New Jersey and changed his name to Noble Drew Ali. He founded the Moorish-American Science Temples. After his death Wallace Ford appeared on the scene claiming to be Ali's reincarnation.

He claimed to have been born in Mecca and was sent to America to redeem the black man from the tyranny of the white man. One of his spokesmen was Elijah Muhammad who helped him found the Nation of Islam and eventually headed the organization.

The most noted leader of the movement was Malcolm X, the mouthpiece of Elijah Muhammad, until he was murdered by one of Muhammad's rivals in 1965. The goal of the Black Muslim movement is to liberate African-Americans from social discrimination and to empower them for self-autonomy. The original leaders also sought to establish a separate nation of African-Americans within the United States. They continue to oppose the integration message of the late Dr. Martin Luther King and other civil rights leaders. Their most outspoken leader today is Louis Farrakan.

Evangelistic Strategy

Be Sensitive To The Muslim Mindset.

Remember how the Muslim person thinks about God and salvation when sharing your faith. They hold to the following basic beliefs:

1. *God cannot be known.* He is transcendent. A verse like John 3:16 contradicts everything a Muslim believes about God.

2. *Religion is external not internal.* Islam focuses on ritual prayer offered five times a day but not intimate communion with God; reflects fearful submission to Allah versus loving obedience to God as Father; and follows religious and moral stipulations without true holiness of life.

3. *Good works provide the pathway to salvation.* However, the only way to fully guarantee entrance into Paradise is through martyrdom for the cause of Islam. The Muslim awaits in his grave the Day of Judgment when his works, not God's grace, will determine his eternal destiny.

4. *While repentance is required, no understanding of God's forgiveness is provided.* Islam offers no doctrine of salvation as the gift of God.

Be Aware Of The Price of Conversion.

The Muslim who converts to Christianity in a strictly Muslim land stands to lose his identity, his family, his livelihood, and possibly his life. Islam extremists view all other religions as satanic in origin.

Be Careful Not To Stereotype All Muslims.

Remember that there are different brands to Islam ranging from moderate to extreme as is true of all religions. One writer observed, "There is an earthshaking struggle under way for the hearts and minds of all Muslims, with large implications for world peace. It is a struggle between those for whom Islam is a faith based on justice, humanism and mercy, and those who preach hatred and violence; between Muslims who wish to see our nations thrive as part of the modern, democratic world, and those would drive us back to the Middle Ages." [4]

To illustrate this point it is interesting to note that during Louis Farrakan's (The Nation of Islam) recent Million Man March, several local Muslim leaders denounced Farrakan's brand of Islam and refused to support the march. The point is that we should be sensitive to the specific orientation of the Muslim person when you minister to them.

Share The Love of God in Word and Deed (Mk 12:29-31).

A close friend of mine, who ministers in Mideastern countries, sat one day in a Syrian restaurant. After placing his order, the waiter said to him, "Can you tell me how to become a Christian?" My friend was stunned believing the waiter to be insincere in his request, thinking he only wanted to get a U.S. visa. So he asked him, "Aren't you a Muslim? Why do you want to convert to Christianity?"

The waiter responded, "I want to become a Christian because yours is the religion of love."

The Christian's secret weapon in evangelism is the love of God. The noted theologian Karl Barth was once asked by a seminary student, "Dr. Barth, what is the greatest statement you can make about the Bible?" He paused, thought for a moment, and then responded, "The greatest statement I can make about the Bible is this—Jesus loves me this I know, for the Bible tells me so."

3

WHAT'S NEW ABOUT NEW AGE?

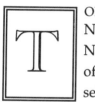ODAY WE HEAR A LOT OF TALK about the New Age. Our bookstores offer a venue of New Age literature. This fast-growing body of literature deals with everything from self-help and spirituality to extraterrestrial travel and spirit possession. Music stores provide a genre of New Age music. Even our politicians speak of a new world order.

What is the New Age movement? Some immediately think of a mix of Shirley McLaine, channelers, crystals, psychics and astrologers. In reality, the New Age movement represents a blending of religious beliefs and occultic practices under one umbrella. Carl A. Raschke, professor of religious studies at the University of Denver, says, "The New Age movement is essentially the maturing of the hippie movement of the 1960s." In many respects New Ageism represents the unification of religion and the human sciences according to the prophetic description of John the Revelator:

> There I saw a woman sitting on a scarlet beast that was covered with blasphemous names...This title was written on her forehead: MYSTERY BABYLON THE GREAT, THE MOTHER OF PROSTITUTES AND OF THE ABOMINATIONS OF THE EARTH. I saw that the woman was drunk with the blood of the saints, the blood of those who bore testimony to Jesus (Rev 17:3,5,6).

Robert Lindsey of the *New York Times* notes:

> According to experts in sociology, religion and psychology...the phenomenon is less a movement than a collection of disparate organizations and iconoclasts challenging orthodox thinking in a wide range of subjects, from religion to physics.
>
> New Age thought, according to many proponents as well as detractors, directly or indirectly rejects the Judeo-Christian concept of a single, omnipotent God Who has revealed His will to man. Instead, New Age adherents follow the view of many Eastern religions that there is a

unity in the universe, of which all things, including God and man, are equal parts. [5]

J. Gordon Melton, director of the Institute for the Study of American Religion in Santa Barbara, California, points out that "since the mid-1960s, there has been a steady increase in openness to metaphysical and occultic ideas in the United States. Beliefs that have existed for a long time on the metaphysical periphery and are now becoming very much part of Middle America." In addition, Fergus M. Bordewich writes: "New Age philosophy is becoming the religion, or at least the ethos, of a growing proportion of the young, professional middle class that is now beginning to move into positions of responsibility and authority in American society." [6]

NEW AGE BELIEFS

World Views

Theism. The Judeo-Christian belief, based on Scripture, reveals one God, eternally existing in three persons (Father, Son and Holy Spirit). God is Creator, Sustainer, Redeemer and Father. God is the ultimate reality, the Absolute of the universe.

Atheism. God does not exist. The universe came about by naturalistic causes and evolutionary processes. Religion is an invention of the unenlightened human intellect.

Pantheism. Pantheism is simply the belief that God and the world are essentially the same. God is not a personal being but is rather the impersonal cosmic power (laws and forces) which binds the whole universe together as one. The earth and all its forces are God. We are God and God is us. The goal of pantheism is to achieve oneness with the universe, or the forces of nature; to live in harmony with nature. Evil and good are myths; there is only order and chaos. The break of oneness is chaos. Reality is not absolute or objective; we create our own reality. Pantheism is the underlying theology of New Ageism.

Views About Life After Death

Annihilation. This view states that nothing happens after death because no reality exists outside the world of space, time and matter.

Resurrection. The Judeo-Christian perspective teaches that the wicked experience eternal judgment and the righteous, eternal life (Dan 12:2; Jn 5:28-29; Rev 20:6, 11-15).

Reincarnation. The New Age belief of reincarnation comes from the ancient eastern religions of Buddhism and Hinduism. Reincarnation regards death as a passage into unending life-cycles. Only perfection can free a person from the unending cycle and lead to nirvana (nothingness) which is loosely defined as one's absorption into eternal reality. The cycle is governed by *karma*—the process of action and reaction or the cosmic law of cause and effect, which states that everyone receives what he or she deserves. One's karma, the sum total of his bad and good deeds, determines the quality of life he enjoys during his next reincarnated life-cycle.

Views About Morality

Morality is absolute. Morals and ethics are rooted in the revelation of God and His law (Ps 19:7-11; 119:89; Matt 4:35; John 17:17).

Morality is relative. Relativism bases moral decisions on situations and personal desires. New Ageism postulates an optimistic view of human nature and rejects the validity of sin and guilt and humanity's subsequent need for atonement. Blaise Pascal, the French scientist noted that, "In a values vacuum, humanity will pursue one of two goals: We will imagine that we ourselves are god or we will seek gratification through our senses." New Ageism in America has driven us in both directions simultaneously.

Views About The Acquisition of Knowledge

Knowledge is attained through reason. Science is the process of attaining knowledge through observation, experimentation and organization. The scientific method involves five steps: (1) define a problem; (2) formulate a hypothesis; (3) test the hypothesis; (4) draw conclusions (empirical evidence); and (5) develop a theory.

Knowledge is attained through revelation. To reveal is to uncover that which is hidden to the five senses; to make known that which was previously unknown. God reveals Himself to us not only through objective reality, but also through the ministry of the Holy Spirit as He speaks to the conscience and to the human spirit (Matt 16:17; Jn 14:16,17,26; 1 Cor 2:6-16).

Knowledge is attained through altered states of consciousness. In the spirit of Eastern mysticism, New Agers promise hidden, secret knowledge to its followers attained through altered states of consciousness. Altered states, ranging from intense concentration to ecstatic trances, are achieved through transcendental meditation, astral projection, contact with spirit guides and ascended masters, centering, yoga, imaging (visualization), channeling, psychic experiences and drug use.

Knowledge is the key to oneness according to New Age beliefs. Those without knowledge still see themselves as individuals as opposed to part of the cosmic whole. Not having yet recognized their divinity, they see life only as fragmented events as opposed to part of an overall master plan into which all the events fit. Reason and belief stand as enemies to enlightenment and need to be eliminated, according to New Ageism.

Views About Jesus Christ

Jesus is the divine Son of God. Christianity claims that Jesus Christ is eternal (Jn 1:1-3), creator (Jn 1:4), incarnate (Jn 1:14), and sinless (2 Cor 5:21). He worked miracles

(Acts 10:38), was crucified for our sins (1 Jn 4:10), was raised for our justification (Rom 4:25), ascended to the right hand of God as our intercessor (Rom 8:31-34), and will return to rule and reign as Lord of all (Rev 19:11-16).

Jesus is an ascended master (Initiate, Guru). New Ageism presents Jesus as one who achieved oneness with ultimate reality like Buddha, Krishna, Elijah, Muhammad, Alexander the Great and others. According to New Age doctrine, Jesus is but one of many Avatars (people sent to show us the way).

The Christ Event represents the moment He achieved godhood and was absorbed back into the ultimate reality of the universe. He was not "the Christ" but "a Christ" because He realized his inherent divinity—a realization every person needs to experience. Every person has the potential for christhood.

Self-esteem, in New Age thought, constitutes the realization of our own inherent divinity. The German mystic Meister Johannes Eckehart (1260-1328) wrote a meditation which reads: "The Lord of love, immortal and infinite, comes as a divine incarnation in times of great crisis to rescue mankind from disaster. Sri Krishna, the Compassionate Buddha, and Jesus the Christ are supreme examples." [7]

The goal of New Age is to strip Jesus of His uniqueness as the Son of God, the Savior of the world, and the King of Kings who possesses all authority in heaven and on earth. The New Age redefines the second coming of Christ merely as the final evolution of human society into the cosmic Christ. Man, not God, creates this utopia, a new world order (the Age of Aquarius) through his own enlightenment.

Views of Sin

Sin is rebellion against God and a transgression of His law. The Bible tells us that sin is: (1) universal (Rom 3:23), (2) a state (Ps 51:5), and (3) an action (Rom 14:23; Jas 4:17; I Jn 3:4; 5:17). Why is there evil in the world? Why is there suffering, war, poverty, crime and death if God made the world and declared it good? Did God create evil? Even worse, is He both good and evil?

Only Genesis explains and accounts for the universal presence of sin in the world. There are two sources of sin: *the Tempter,* who slandered the character of God and promised Adam and Eve that if they ate of the fruit they would be like God with full knowledge; and *human choice* (Gen 2:16; 3:6,7). God placed Adam ("man") and Eve ("living"), the parents of us all, in the garden to work and take care of it. God told them, "You are free to eat from any tree in the garden; but you must not eat from the tree of the knowledge of good and evil, for when you eat of it you will surely die" (Gen 2:16).

The Hebrew words for good and evil are *tob* and *ra,* meaning the pleasure and the pain. The issue was whether or not they would trust God's wisdom about good and evil or go their own way. Herein lies the essence of sin—we reject God's way to go our own way.

Three vital lessons are learned from the Fall:

1. *The Fall refutes evolution.* Instead of starting at the bottom and evolving to the top, we started at the top and fell to the bottom.

2. *The Fall refutes humanism.* Humanism asserts that man is basically good. It is the environment which conditions him to be bad. The reality, however, is that man was tested in a perfect environment. Our problem is not external but internal, "For all have sinned and come short of the glory of God" (Rom 3:23).

3. *The Fall teaches that man is a responsible being.* He is subject to God. He is not independent of God. The command, "You shall not eat it," underscores man's dependency on God for morality and truth. The command defines our relationship as one of responsibility to God for our moral choices. Sin consists of resisting God's will, rejecting God's word, and departing from God's way. The only antidote for sin is the redemption provided by Jesus Christ through His death, resurrection, and ascension. Romans 3:24 tells us that we are "justified freely by His grace through the redemption that came by Jesus Christ."

Sin is a myth. In contrast to the biblical doctrine of sin, new ageism states that evil is an illusion. The concept of sin presupposes an absolute authority or will which is transgressed. Since New Ageism accepts no such moral absolute, sin cannot exist. This being the case, man does not need a Redeemer because he is not a sinner.

DISTINCTIVE FEATURES ─────────────────────────

While it is difficult to nail down a succinct definition of the New Age, certain distinctive features emerge:

1. The God of the New Age is an impersonal force within all creation. God is all, and all is God.
2. Man is god who consists of and creates the forces of life. Man only needs to awaken to the creative powers residing within him.
3. Man should seek and accept spiritual enlightenment directly from the spirit world through the process of altered states of consciousness. Contact with the dead and with spirit guides is sought.
4. All religions lead to the same goal. All have equal merit. New Ageism borrows heavily from Christian terminology but distorts the true meaning of Christian beliefs and values.
5. The ancient wisdom of Babylon, Egypt, and Greece—not the Bible—provides the basis of truth. The highest virtue is what feels right. This fosters sociopathic personalities which believe everything is permissible.
6. New Ageism parts company not only with Christianity but also with science. Its validation of mystical and magical experience casts a shadow of doubt over rational thought. Its denial of the past as a basis for action separates people from both their own and society's

history. Spiritual fable is elevated on objective reality.

7. New Ageism influences political, social, educational, economic and religious institutions. It is associated with the human potential movement in humanistic psychology, holistic health, astrology, channeling, deep ecology (rejects the view that nature seeks to serve humanity), feminism (goddess worship) and parapsychology (ESP, psychic phenomena, out of body experiences). Many major corporations now offer New Age workshops designed to help employees handle stress, develop healthier relationships, and produce productivity.

8. Metaphysical techniques including yoga, meditation, releasing, centering, and crystals are used to combat illness, manage stress and achieve happiness. What we think, we become. We create our own reality through higher levels of consciousness.

9. New Ageism travels with the occult in its use of crystals, tarot cards, ouija boards and witchcraft. Witchcraft has been re-packaged as a positive force for social change, detaching itself openly from such concepts of Satanism.

10. New Ageism emphasizes globalism and the dethronement of national sovereignty. The concept of oneness has political implications which set the stage for the Antichrist spirit expressed in a global economy, a global government, a

global military and police force, and a global religion.

New Ageism represents the consummation of Satan's lie to Adam and Eve—"You will be like God, knowing good and evil" (Gen 3:5). The appeal lies in its denial of original sin and human guilt, its elevation of humanity to deity, its freedom from responsibility before God and others, and its empowerment of people with feelings of superiority. Like all Satan's lies, there is only pleasure in sin for a short time. What we really long for is not to be God, but to know God personally and intimately (Ps 16:11). As Saint Augustine prayed, "Our hearts were made for Thee, O God, and they shall not rest until they rest in Thee."

FROM NEW AGE TO NEW BIRTH

The testimony of Sharon Beekman underscores not only the dangers of New Age, but most importantly, the liberating power of the new birth:

> The evil within and around me manipulated my body, emotions and thoughts much as a cat playing with a half-dead mouse. The problem had started in 1977, when I began exploring psychic phenomena and the spiritual realm. In meditation class at a spiritualist church, I learned to be a channel for spirits. I also studied the I-Ching, acupressure, Tarot, Native American and Eastern

spirituality, astrology and the Seth books. I established a ritual of yoga and meditation an hour each morning.

By 1985 I had difficulty completing thoughts, lacked emotion and lived in isolation. I was a poor reflection of the vibrant, successful mental health professional I once had been.

I decided to stop channeling. It was then the spirits revealed their true nature. I called Tad, a Christian friend from college, and described my situation...My harassment worsened after I received the materials from Tad. Finally, one night I sobbed, "I've got to find a Christian...I need Jesus Christ."

In the spring of 1987, acting on Tad's advice, I called an inner-city church. "I'm demon-possessed," I said, "and would like to know Jesus Christ. Could someone there help me?"

Without hesitating, the church secretary said, "Yes, we would love to talk with you. Come right down!"

After introductions, the young pastor and a woman from the congregation bowed their heads and prayed. They sounded like children appealing to a loving father. Their love for God impressed me. I longed to love in that way.

As he described God's love for me, the spirits screamed objections in my mind. But I knew they lied. "What do I need to do?" I asked.

"Well, Sharon...Romans 10:9 says, 'If you confess with your mouth, 'Jesus is Lord,' and believe in your heart that God raised him from the dead, you will be saved'."

Eagerly I prayed aloud, "Lord Jesus Christ, I confess that I have sinned against you. Please forgive me. I want You to be Lord and Savior of my life. Amen." As they continued praying, I felt the Spirit of God fill the cold place at my center.

Every week for the next year, I attended church services, participated in a Bible study, and prayed with the pastor and lay minister. I also emptied my house of all paraphernalia associated with the occult and New Age thinking.

I called my friend Tad. "Jesus quieted my mind," I told her, "but do you know the greatest miracle of all?...He's changing me! That sense of emptiness is gone and I feel loved, really loved, and I genuinely love others. What a miracle!" [8]

4

JUDAISM AND JESUS

"Do not think that I have come to destroy
the Law or the Prophets; I have not come
to abolish them but to fulfill them."
- Jesus (Matthew 5:17)

 HE TERM *JUDAISM,* FROM THE GREEK word
Ioudaismos, refers to the religion and culture
of the Jewish people. The word first appeared
during the intertestamental period by
Greek-speaking Jews to distinguish their way
of life and belief from that of the Greeks.

Abraham was the father of the Hebrew nation. The
word *Hebrew* is an English equivalent of the word *Habiru*
meaning wanderer or sojourner, referring to the nomadic
lifestyle of the Patriarchs. The later term *Jew* originally
referred to those belonging to the tribe of Judah but later
came to refer to anyone of the Hebrew race.

The history of the Jewish people is one marked by the fingerprints of God. They have endured rejection, invasion, captivity, and dispersion, yet they occupy center-stage in contemporary history. God's covenant to Abraham still stands:

> I will make you into a great nation and I will bless you; I will make your name great, and you will be a blessing. I will bless those who bless you, and whoever curses you I will curse; and all peoples on earth will be blessed through you (Gen 12:2,3).

During the reign of the Russian Czar Peter the Great, an elderly preacher was imprisoned for his faith. The Czar summoned him one day and asked, "Can you give me one infallible proof to verify the Bible?" "Yes, Sire," he replied, "the Jew." Former President Harry Truman said that the most important action he performed while in office was to sign the agreement recognizing Israel as an Independent State.

HISTORICAL DEVELOPMENTS

Jewish history is, in reality, a story of faith. Their history can be traced along the following dateline:

- 2,000 B.C.   The call of Abraham from Ur of Chaldees to the Promised Land.

- 1,450 B.C.   The Exodus under the leadership of Moses.
- 1,400 B.C.   Joshua leads the conquest of Canaan.
- 1,380 B.C.   The period of the Judges for 330 years.
- 1,053 B.C.   Saul inaugurated as the first Israeli King.
- 1,013 B.C.   The Davidic Kingdom established and the covenant given.
- 930 B.C.   Israel divided after Solomon's death.
- 722 B.C.   Israel (northern kingdom) invaded by Assyria and exiled.
- 586 B.C.   Judah (southern kingdom) invaded by Babylon and exiled.
- 539 B.C.   Jews returned to Jerusalem after 70 years of Babylonian captivity.
- 165 B.C.   Jews rededicate temple after defeating Syrians (Hanukkah).
- 63 B.C.   Rome rises to power and controls Israel.
- 70 A.D.   Rome destroys Jerusalem and temple under Titus (Massada).
- 135 A.D.   Hadrian the Roman invades Israel and renames it *Palestine.*
- 1882 A.D.   First group of Jewish colonists settle in Palestine.
- 1914 A.D.   England, France, and Russia declare war on Ottoman Turks.

- 1917 A.D.   Forces under General Allenby advance into Palestine.
- 1918 A.D.   The Balfour Declaration signed. British guarantee Jewish state.
- 1948 A.D.   United Nations recognizes Israel as an Independent State.
- 1948 A.D.   War of Independence fought against five Arab states.
- 1956 A.D.   Sinai Campaign fought against Egypt, Jordan and Syria.
- 1967 A.D.   Six Day War resulting in Jews recapturing Jerusalem.
- 1973 A.D.   Yom Kippur (Day of Atonement) War.
- 1995 A.D.   Peace Treaty signed between Israel and Syria.

Throughout the biblical period the Jewish religion developed through a series of stages including the Patriarchs (Genesis), the Mosaic Period and the Law, the Intertestamental Period, the Rabbinical Period (during Christ's time), the Medieval Period, and the Modern Period. The result today is a unified Jewish faith consisting of diverse sects including *Orthodox* (strict adherence to law and tradition), *Reformed* (or Neo-Orthodox, reaction to orthodoxy), *Conservative* (blend of orthodox and reformed) and *Messianic* (those who accept Jesus as Israel's Messiah). Perhaps the essence of Judaism is still embodied in one prophetic call to "act justly, to love mercy and to walk humbly with your God" (Micah 6:8).

FUNDAMENTALS OF FAITH

The source of Jewish religious belief derives from two primary sources: the Old Testament, especially the Mosaic Law (*Torah*), and the Talmud. The Talmud consists of oral tradition and law developed during the intertestamental period which reflects the primary religion of the rabbis. It includes the *Mishna*, a written record of oral law dated A.D. 200 and edited by Rabbi Judah ha-Nasi, and the *Gemara*, a rabbinical commentary on the Mishna, completed in A.D. 500. The

He spoke as the Son of God.

Talmud consists of over 6,000 folio pages and is the work of over 2,000 scholars.

Judaism reflects theological diversity as seen in the differences between the Pharisees, Sadducees and Essenes even in the time of Christ. Traditionally, more emphasis has been placed on *deed* (*miswa*) than the *creed* (*ani ma'amin*, "I believe"). The Mishna (Abot 1:2) presents a broad philosophy characteristic of the early rabbis: "By three things is the world sustained: by the law, by the [temple] service and by deeds of lovingkindness."

This basic premise is supported by the three-fold purpose of the synagogue which exists as a house of *study* (to learn the Torah), a house of *prayer* (to worship God), and a house of *assembly* (to cultivate community life). This description parallels the role of the Church which exists to proclaim the *Word of God*, to *worship* God and to seek the *welfare* of the community in both the household of faith and the world.

Four foundational pillars, interacting with one another, provide the essence of covenant life: (1) *the Torah* (law), always a living law as the written Torah is understood in light of the oral Torah; (2) *one God*, who is spiritual and eternal; (3) *the people of Israel*, who exist as one family with a corporate personality; and (4) *the land*, which originates in God's promise to Abraham.

The fundamentals of Judaism as a way of life can be summarized as follows:

- Man is pivotal in the universe as a partner with God in the unending process of creation. In rabbinical thought, "God needs man as much as man needs God."
- Man is a responsible moral agent, free to make his own choices, yet ultimately accountable to God.
- Human progress is achieved through the actualization of human potential. The nature of man is essentially good, capable of rising above the tendencies of sin. Thus he can be hopeful and optimistic about his future.

- Judaism focuses more on life "here-and-now" versus "then-and-there" in eternity. Earth and man constitute a greater concern than God and heaven. Thoughts about life after death have never occupied a major position in Jewish thought.
- All of life is sacred. Man is to seek the imitation of God in sanctifying every area of his life.
- Man is to seek peace, justice and righteousness; themes which occupy a central place in the Old Testament. We are responsible to improve society through good deeds. While traditional Judaism views the Messiah as God's anointed human representative who will usher in a golden age of spiritual and social redemption, reformed Judaism teaches that the Messianic Age will transpire when humankind reaches a level of enlightenment, peace and justice. [9]

THE JESUS FACTOR

Where does Jesus fit in with Judaism? First of all, Jesus was a Jew born a descendant of King David through the lineage of Joseph and Mary (Matt 1:1-16; Lk 3:23-37). Paul focuses on Jesus' Jewish ancestry when he describes the privileges of Israel (Rom 9:4,5).

During His ministry, Jesus was recognized as a Rabbi and given the honor and privilege afforded that standing. His preaching and teaching ministries focused on the synagogues (Matt 4:23). Other rabbinical leaders confirmed his rabbinical authority and accepted the validity of His miracles (Jn 3:1,2). Some were even His secret disciples (Lk 23:50-52; Jn 7:50-52; 19:38-42).

His teaching captivated all who heard Him. "Never spake a man like this man," the temple guards remarked on one occasion (Jn 7:47). "The people were amazed at his teaching, because he taught them as one having authority, not as the teachers of the law" (Mk 1:22). The authority with which He spoke separated Jesus from the other rabbinical teachers of His day. Even the chief priests and elders recognized His authority and questioned its source: "'By what authority are you doing these things?' they asked. 'And who gave you this authority?'" (Matt 21:23).

Scripture over tradition.

What constituted His authority? First, He spoke as the Son of God. In the Gospels Jesus is called *"the Son of God"* 49 times, the *"Only Begotten Son"* five times, *"My Son"* 10 times, *"the Son"* 34 times, *"His Son"* 24 times, and *"the Son of Man"* (a messianic title) 86 times. Jesus openly confessed His deity and received the worship of the people (Matt 2:2; 21:1-11; 28:9,17). He declared, "Before Abraham was born, I am!" which nearly got Him stoned because He claimed equality with God (Jn 8:58,59).

The phrase "I Am" comes from the burning bush experience of Moses (Ex 3:14). From that experience Moses identified the God of Israel by His covenant name *Yahweh*, meaning the Promise Keeper. Jesus said "I Am" the Messiah (Jn 4:26), the Bread of Life (Jn 6:35), the Light of the World (Jn 8:12), the Gate for the Sheep (Jn 10:7), the Good Shepherd (Jn 10:11), the Son of God (Jn 10:36), the Resurrection and the Life (Jn 11:25), and the True Vine (Jn 15:1).

Jesus and The Law

His authority also derived from His emphasis on the Scripture as authoritative over oral tradition. He condemned the elevation of rabbinical tradition to the superior level of the Scripture. Listen to His challenge to the rabbinical leaders:

> And why do you break the command of God for the sake of your tradition?...Thus you nullify the word of God for the sake of your tradition. You hypocrites! Isaiah was right when he prophesied about you: "These people honor me with their lips, but their hearts are far from me. They worship me in vain; their teachings are but rules taught by men" (Matt 15:3,6,7).

Jesus stressed the sole authority of the Old Testament and refuted the authority of oral rabbinical teaching which held the people in bondage to a legalistic system of rules. "You are in error," He told the Sadducees, "because you do not know the Scriptures or the power of God" (Matt 22:29).

Jesus never took issue with the Old Testament; rather, He upheld its teachings and sought to clarify the Scripture because its true meaning had been buried under a pile of rabbinical tradition. Consequently, the people could not distinguish between God's truth in Scripture and the traditions of the rabbis. This is what Jesus meant when He said, "Do not think that I have come to abolish the Law or the Prophets; I have not come to abolish them but to fulfill them" (Matt 5:17).

Jesus summed up the Law and Prophets in two great commands: "Love the Lord your God with all your heart, mind, soul, and strength" (Deut 6:4), and "Love your neighbor as yourself" (Lev 19:18). The true goal of Judaism, then, is to live in right relationship with God and man. This, of course, is the essence of the Christian gospel which reconciles man to God and man to man through Jesus Christ.

Jesus and Salvation

Jesus echoed the truth of salvation stated clearly in the Old Testament. Salvation does not come through keeping the Law—either the law of God or the tradition of the rabbis. The Pharisees, during the Intertestamental Period, were the first to teach that entrance into the kingdom of God required one to know the law and keep the law in contrast. The Old Testament sets forth the truth that we are saved from our sins through faith in the grace of God, not by good works or ritualistic observances.

Listen to what Jesus told a Pharisee named Nicodemus about salvation:

> "I tell you the truth, no one can see the kingdom of God unless he is born again (or "born from above")"..."How can a man be born a second time?" he asked. Jesus responded, "Just as Moses lifted up the snake in the desert, so the Son of Man must be lifted up, that everyone who believes in him may have eternal life" (Jn 3:3,14,15, parenthesis added).

The uplifted snake which Moses used in the wilderness symbolized God's judgment against sin through a substitutionary offering. This same imagery appears throughout the Old Testament as seen in God's covering of Adam and Eve, the ram provided on Moriah in Isaac's place, the Passover Lamb in Egypt, and the annual Day of Atonement. Our response is to believe, to trust, to put our faith in the loving provision of God who alone redeems us from our sins. The way of salvation by faith is seen in Abraham, the father of the Jewish nation, who "believed the Lord, and he credited it to him as righteousness" (Gen 15:6).

Judaism did not begin as a religion of law, it began as a religion of faith as seen in Abraham. The law was added to provide the new nation established under Moses' leadership a system of government, morality, and worship. The purpose of the law, however, was never to make men right with God. Nowhere in the Old Testament is such a notion presented. Paul reminded us that "the law was put in charge to lead us to Christ that we might be justified by faith" (Gal 3:24). The Old Testament prophet Habakkuk agreed with Paul when he declared, "the righteous will live by his faith" (Hab 2:4).

Jesus and the Sacrifices
Not only did the Law not make men righteous, neither did the sacrificial system of the temple worship. Old Testament sacrifices, in and of themselves, did not atone for sins just as receiving the Lord's Supper does not atone for sins. Confession, repentance and faith result in the forgiveness of sins (1 Jn 1:9).

Both the Old Testament sacrifices and the Eucharist illustrate atonement and provide avenues for the expression of faith; but they remain the means of grace, not grace itself. Atonement is the work of God who alone redeems us from our sins. The redemption of Israel from Egypt clearly underscores this truth. The Exodus demonstrates God's grace which redeemed His people by His power and the blood of the Passover Lamb. Redemption, then, came by power and blood. The very act of putting the blood of the Passover lamb on the door posts was an act of faith on Israel's part in what God would do on their behalf.

Offering sacrifices without personal confession of sin and faith in God was condemned by the prophets throughout the Old Testament. Samuel said, "Obedience is better than sacrifice" (1 Sam 15:22). When David repented of his sin with Bathsheba, he prayed, "You do not delight in sacrifice, or I would bring it; you do not take pleasure in burnt offerings. The sacrifices of God are a broken spirit; a broken and contrite heart, O God, you will not despise" (Ps 51:16,17).

The psalmist Asaph proclaimed the word of God to Israel by asking: "Do I eat the flesh of bulls or drink the blood of goats? Sacrifice thank offerings to God, fulfill your vows to the Most High, and call upon me in the day of trouble; I will deliver you, and you will honor me" (Ps 50:13-15). Isaiah condemned Israel's sacrificial system when it was practiced without personal repentance and social justice: "Stop bringing meaningless offerings!" (Isa 1:13). Jeremiah rebuked the people in his day for trusting in the temple service yet living in unbelief and disobedience (Jer 7:1-15).

> *Atonement is the work of God who alone redeems us.*

The five major Levitical offerings which taught true repentance before God and man include:

- the burnt offering (Lev 1:1-17);
- the grain offering (Lev 2:1-16);
- the fellowship (peace) offering (Lev 3:1-17);
- the sin offering (Lev 4:1-5:13); and
- the guilt (trespass) offering (Lev 5:14-6:7).

These offerings did not save; God's grace received by faith and repentance saved the worshippers. This is the essence of the Christian gospel which fulfills Judaism. Jesus is the fulfillment of the sacrificial system. The last Old Testament prophet John the Baptist said of Jesus, "Behold the Lamb of God who takes away the sin of the world" (Jn 1:29). Paul adds, "Christ, our Passover Lamb, has been sacrificed" (1 Cor 5:7).

Jesus often spoke of the necessity of His death as the fulfillment of the sacrificial system; a sacrifice spoken of throughout the Old Testament. On one occasion He said, "For the Son of Man did not come to be served, but to serve, and to give his life as a ransom for many" (Mk 10:45).

Isaiah declared of the Messiah,

He was pierced for our transgressions, he was crushed for our iniquities; the punishment that brought us peace was upon him, and by his wounds we are healed. We all, like sheep, have gone astray, each of us has turned to his own way; and the Lord has laid on him the iniquity of us all (Isa 53:5,6).

Who is this sin-bearer? Who is this Passover lamb who has borne the iniquity of us all, Jew and Gentile alike? The rabbinical tradition teaches that this prophecy refers to the persecution and oppression suffered by the Israeli nation with specific reference to the Babylonian exile.

Jesus, however, announced its fulfillment in His crucifixion. After His resurrection He told the disciples: "Everything must be fulfilled that is written about me in the Law of Moses, the Prophets and the Psalms." Then He opened their minds so they could understand the Scriptures. He told them, "This is what is written: The Christ will suffer and rise from the dead on the third day, and repentance and forgiveness of sins will be preached in his name to all nations, beginning at Jerusalem" (Lk 24:44-47).

Jesus and the Covenants

The following covenants can be identified in Scripture:

- the Edenic (Gen 1:28);
- the Adamaic (Gen 3:15);
- the Noahic (Gen 9:10);
- the Abrahamic (Gen 15:18);
- the Mosaic (Ex 19:25);
- the Palestinian (Deut 30:3);
- the Davidic (2 Sam 7:16); and
- the New Covenant (Jer 31:31-34).

Four covenants are eternal: the Abrahamic, the Palestinian, the Davidic and the New Covenants. They are based on God's grace and secured by His own eternal decree. As such these covenants are unalterable. These covenants are literal, unconditional and provisional for Israel and the nations of the world as they reveal God's plan of redemption.

The Abrahamic covenant promises a *seed* and a *land* to Israel. The Palestinian covenant expounds on the land promises of the Abrahamic covenant.

The Davidic covenant promises a *house,* a *kingdom* and a *throne* for David's descendant's throughout eternity. The Old Testament prophets viewed the eternal throne of David as the Messiah's throne (Jer 23:5,6; 30:8,9; 33:14-17, 20-21; Ezek 37:24,25; Dan 7:13,14; Hos 3:4,5; Amos 9:11; Zech 14:4,9). Isaiah's prophecy of the Messiah's kingdom is without question the fulfillment of the Davidic covenant:

> For unto us a child is born, unto us a son is given: and the government shall be upon his shoulder: and his name shall be called Wonderful, Counselor, the Mighty God, the Everlasting Father, the Prince of Peace. Of the increase of his government there shall be no end, upon the throne of David, and upon his kingdom to order it, and to establish it with judgment and with justice from henceforth even forever. The zeal of the Lord of hosts will perform this (Isa 9:6,7).

The New Covenant provides salvation for sin through the grace of God. As the establisher of the New Covenant, Jesus fulfills the previous covenants as the promised Messiah for Israel and the world (Matt 26:26-30; Heb 8:7-13).

Why did the Old Covenant need to be superseded by the New Covenant of Christ? While the Old Testament sacrifices reminded worshipers of their sins (Heb 10:1-4), only Christ's sacrifice can cleanse the conscience of the worshiper enabling him to come before God with confidence (Heb 4:14-16; 9:11-15; 10:11-18). The Old Covenant was *external*, based on ritualism, *powerless*, reflecting the peoples' inability to keep the law, and *temporary*, reflecting God's plan for the old to give way to the new. The writer of Hebrews underscores the finality of the New Covenant of Jesus:

> But God found fault with the people and said: "The time is coming," declares the Lord, "when I will make a new covenant..." by calling this covenant "new," He has made the first one obsolete; and what is obsolete and aging will soon disappear. For this reason Christ is the mediator of a new covenant, that those who are called may receive the promised eternal inheritance (Heb 8:8,13; 9:15).

Jesus and Prophecy

Jesus is the fulfillment of all God's promises in the Old Testament. He is the goal of the Old Testament law, sacrifice, temple service, covenants, prophecy and Messianic hope. Everything points to Him and finds its fulfillment in Him.

It is has been noted that Jesus fulfilled some 300 Old Testament prophecies in His coming. Consider a few:

- Gen 12:3   Born the seed of Abraham

- 2 Sam 7:12   Born the seed of King David
- Micah 5:2   Born in Bethlehem
- Isa 7:14   Born of a virgin
- Isa 9:1,7   A light for the Gentiles
- Isa 11:1   Called a Nazarene
- Isa 53:5   Suffered rejection
- Isa 53:9   Buried with the rich
- Zech 9:9   Triumphal entry on a donkey
- Zech 11:12   Betrayed for 30 pieces of silver
- Ps 22:18   Garments gambled for at crucifixion
- Ps 22:1   Prayed, "My God, why have you forsaken me?"
- Ps 34:10   Not a bone was broken in his body at the cross
- Ps 16:10   Raised from the dead
- Ps 24:7-10   Ascended into heaven

The Apostle John wrote: "The testimony of Jesus is the spirit of prophecy" (Rev 19:10). A Jewish Christian in my former congregation gave me a note after a worship service which read: "I once read in the Jewish Talmud: 'The Law and the Prophets speak of nothing but Messiah and his kingdom.'"

ISRAEL AND THE CHURCH

The identity of the New Testament church is rooted in the history and purpose of Israel in the plan of God. In the

Old Testament Israel is referred to as "a nation of priests" (Ex 19:6) while in the New Testament the Church is called a "royal priesthood, a holy nation" (1 Pt 2:9). Furthermore, the Church is referred to as the new Israel of God in the New Testament (Gal 6;16). This does not mean that God has abandoned His plan for the nation of Israel; He has not. However, the covenant of Abraham promised a blessing for "all nations."

The following New Testament passages compare Israel and the Church:

- Gentiles in Christ are branches grafted into Israel the vine (Rom 11:17).
- Christ destroyed the dividing wall between Jews and Gentiles, making one new man out of the two (Eph 2:11-18).
- Believers in Jesus are children of Abraham and heirs of the promise (Gal 3:6,7,11,26).
- The true Jew is one who is circumcised in his heart not just in the flesh; for not all who are descended from Israel are Israel (Rom 2:28,29; 9:6).
- The Church was addressed as "the Israel of God" (Gal 6:16), and "the twelve tribes scattered among the nations" (Jas 1:1).
- The complete redeemed community of both Old and New Testament saints was pictured in the Revelation as 24 elders (Rev 4:10), 144,000 Jews (Rev 7:4-8; 14:1-5), and the New Jerusalem with

the names of the 12 tribes of Israel and the 12 apostles of Christ (Rev 21:1-5, 12-14).

- The prophets foretold the grafting of the Gentiles into the covenant (Hos 1:10; 2:23).

Originally, first century Jewish Christians worshipped in the synagogues. Christianity was simply regarded as a sect of Judaism called "the Way" (Acts 9:2). Christianity and Judaism parted company due to the persecution of Christians, launched initially by Saul of Tarsus. Later Christianity became more heavily identified with Gentiles who readily accepted the Gospel.

In many respects the commission of the Church corresponds to God's call to Israel. God chose Israel:

- to witness the one true God in the midst of paganism (Deut 6:4,5);
- to demonstrate the blessings of serving and obeying God (Ps 144:15);
- to preserve the word of God from generation to generation (Ps 145:1-7);
- to prepare for the coming of Messiah (Isa 40:1-3);
- to live a holy life in priestly ministry (Ex 19:6; Lev 11:45); and
- to model the love of God for all nations (Gen 12:1-3).

David, who was appointed governor of

ʌlthough the city of Jerusalem was restored and the temple rebuilt, it soon became apparent that Zerubbabel was not another David and the hope for Messiah was projected into the future. Eventually it would be projected in the far and distant future to the end of the age.

This became the prevailing mood of the messianic expectation as seen in the later Old Testament writings. Jeremiah foretold a continuation of the Davidic line (Jer 33), Isaiah prophesied the glory of the coming king (Isa 9,11), Micah announced the birth of the Davidic king in Bethlehem (Mic 5:2), and Zechariah described the character of the messianic kingdom (Zech 9,12). However, these prophecies were more than the reflection of mere human hope, they were the prophetic voice of God which found fulfillment in the angelic announcement to Mary regarding her miraculous conception: "give him the name Jesus. He will be great and will be called the Son of the Most High. The Lord God will give him the throne of his father David, and he will reign over the house of Jacob forever; his kingdom will never end" (Luke 1:31b-33).

During the intertestamental period several different interpretations of the Messianic profile developed. Most importantly, many believed two Messiahs would appear; a Davidic Messiah who would rule as king, and a Levitical Messiah who would serve as priest. By the latter portion of the intertestamental period the prominent belief was only in a Davidic Messiah.

What would this Davidic Messiah be like? We get a description of him in Psalm 17 of the Apocryphal book, *Psalms of Solomon*. First, he will be a human figure who serves as an earthly king over the nation of Israel championing her cause in world affairs.

Second, the title "Messiah" will first be used in a technical sense indicating that at that point the title itself and the messianic concept have been merged together. Third, the Messiah will be upright in all his ways and his hope will be in the Lord. Fourth, his kingdom will be an earthly kingdom with Jerusalem as its capital which will endure forever.

This description became the messianic expectation throughout the remainder of the intertestamental period and lived on in the first century of the Christian era. During the time of Christ the Messianic Kingdom had become a composite picture derived from Old Testament and apocryphal sources. The people's expectation of the kingdom included the following:

- Elijah would return to be the forerunner of the Messiah.
- The Messianic Age would begin with the travail of the Messiah.
- The New Age would be a time of terror at the Day of the Lord, a time of cosmic upheaval, and a time of complete disintegration of the universe itself and all relationships.
- It would be a time of divine judgment.

- Gentile nations would either be judged or redeemed depending upon different theological perspectives.
- There would be an in-gathering of Israel back to her homeland from all nations.
- Jerusalem would be restored and given a new Temple.
- The dead would be raised.
- The New Age of the Kingdom would endure forever.
- A complete restoration of all things would occur including a reuniting of the divided kingdom, abundant agricultural fertility, the end of all war and strife, peace between man and the animal kingdom, the removal of all sickness, pain, sorrow and death, and a climax of holiness and righteousness. [10]

By the dawn of the Christian era the vast majority of the Jews shared the belief in the coming of a mighty Messiah-warrior of David's line. The Qumran Covenanters and the Zealots shared this view and were eagerly anticipating him coming to free them from the Roman yoke of oppression.

This explains why Jesus did not refer to Himself as Messiah and encouraged others to refrain from using the title of Him. He knew He was the Messiah and so did his disciples (Mark 8:29). But not until His trial before Caiaphas, the High Priest, did he openly declare Himself as the Messiah (Mark 14:61,62).

The reason for this is clear: the people expected the Messiah to usher in a political-military kingdom by force. But Jesus understood the Messianic mission as one of establishing the kingdom of God spiritually in the hearts of all people. The kingdom of God would only come through His crucifixion, resurrection, and ascension.

At Caesarea Phillipi, where Peter made the confession, "You are the Christ (Messiah), the Son of the Living God," Jesus, "warned His disciples not to tell anyone that He was the Christ (Messiah)." Furthermore, "From that time on Jesus began to explain to His disciples that He must go to Jerusalem and suffer many things...be killed and on the third day be raised to life" (Matt 16:16-21).

Jesus connected His messiahship with His redemptive work as the crucified Savior. His messianic ministry was based on the necessity of His suffering for the sins of the world (Mark 10:45). According to the Jewish perspective the deliverance which the Son of Man would bring was not salvation from sin, but deliverance from oppressive enemy nations.

Jesus' Kingdom Message
It was this environment, where the Jewish people longed for a Messiah to deliver them from Roman oppression and to establish the Davidic kingdom of old, into which Jesus was born, grew and ministered. While he deliberately avoided the title *Messiah,* He spoke freely of Himself as the Son of Man, and boldly announced that by His very presence in the world, "The Kingdom of God is at hand."

When Jesus announced the kingdom, He caught the attention of everyone in Israel. His kingdom message rang out as a message of hope. There existed a high level of Messianic expectation among the people who envisioned a kingdom of vast economic, political and military resources which would overthrow Rome and usher in the glory of the Davidic kingdom. Such expectation was in order. For centuries Israel suffered subjection to Gentile world powers even as the prophet Daniel foresaw in his apocalyptic visions: Babylon (605 BC), Medo-Persia (539 BC), Greece (333 BC) and Rome (63 BC).

Rome placed a puppet king over Israel named Herod who was an Idumean (an Edomite descendant). Israel existed as a Roman territory. The Antonio Fortress where Pilate ruled as governor was constructed next to the Temple. Roman authority controlled Herod and the temple party of the Sadducees (priests). Israel was so heavily taxed that much of the land existed in abject poverty. Needless to say it was a time of darkness—economically, socially, politically, but most of all spiritually. The people longed for Isaiah's Messiah to appear (Isa 9:1-7).

To a hopeless and desperate people Jesus announced the immediacy of the kingdom of God. No wonder they flocked to hear Him by the multitudes. The most important truth He spoke about the kingdom was: "The kingdom is within you" (Lk 17:20,21).

His kingdom would not come with military might, political power or religious aristocracy. His kingdom would not be measured by lands conquered, subjects and slaves, wealth and power. His kingdom would not be centered in the Holy City Jerusalem, on the seven hills of Rome, or in Babylon. His kingdom would be established in the hearts of everyone who believed on Him and followed Him: "To all who received him, to those who believed in his name, he gave the right to become children of God" (Jn 1:12).

Not only did He announce the arrival of the Kingdom, He embodied the kingdom, and demonstrated it by driving out demons, healing the sick, and performing miracles (Matt 4:17-25). Such was the meaning of His statement, "But if I drive out demons by the Spirit of God, then the kingdom of God has come upon you" (Matt 12:28).

The Messianic Secret

While Jesus openly declared and demonstrated the kingdom, He also spoke of its mystery element. During a series of kingdom parables He was teaching to a crowd, He privately told His disciples, "The secret of the kingdom of God has been given to you" (Mark 4:11). This *Messianic secret* consisted of the manner in which the kingdom of God would come—not through military force or a political insurrection but rather through His suffering on the cross, His resurrection from the dead, His ascension to heaven and the subsequent coming of the Holy Spirit. His resurrection would inaugurate the coming of the kingdom with power (Mark 9:1; Rom 1:4). After which the secret of redemption would be openly proclaimed "as a witness to all nations" (Matt 24:14).

The cross was the "secret of the kingdom." As such it was part of the predetermined counsel of God. In the crucifixion the Son of Man became the Suffering Servant of the Lord. Jesus saw in Himself the prophetic fulfillment of both Daniel's Son of Man (Dan 7:13,14) and Isaiah's Suffering Servant (Isa 53:1-12).

As the church began its ministry in the world after Jesus' ascension, it proclaimed the Messiahship of Jesus (Acts 2:36) and the present reality of the kingdom of God (Acts 28:31) which is entered through faith in Jesus (Jn 3:3).

> *"The Kingdom is Within You."*
> *— Jesus*

Not only is the kingdom a present reality but it is also the blessed hope of the church. Jesus will return and consummate the kingdom: "The kingdom of the world has become the kingdom of our Lord and of his Christ, and he will reign for ever and ever" (Rev 11:15). When Christ returns, all the prophecies about the Messianic kingdom will be fulfilled.

ISRAEL IN BIBLE PROPHECY

The modern rebirth of Israel is one of the most important prophecies to be fulfilled in our time pointing to the return of Christ. What will be the final destiny of Israel? The Apostle Paul foresaw the day of Israel's salvation as he echoed the words of the prophet Isaiah: "The deliverer will come from Zion; he will turn godlessness away from Jacob. And this is my covenant with them when I take away their sins" (Rom 11:26,27). He goes on to say, in regard to Israel, that "God's gifts and his call are irrevocable" (11:29). God's purpose and plan for Israel continues today as He prepares Her and the world for Messiah's coming.

The prophet Isaiah gives us a preview of Christ's return and Israel's place in the Messianic Kingdom:

> The people will say, "Come let us go up to the mountain of the Lord, to the house of the God of Jacob. He will teach us His ways, so that we may walk in His paths. The law will go out from Zion, the word of the Lord from Jerusalem."
>
> They will beat their swords into plowshares and their spears into pruning hooks. Nation will not take up sword against nation, nor will they train for war anymore.
>
> The wolf and the lamb will feed together and the lion will eat straw like an ox. They will neither harm nor destroy on all my holy mountain, says the Lord.
>
> For the earth will be full of the knowledge of the Lord as the waters cover the sea (Isa 2:3,4; 11:9; 65:25).

THE CHRISTIAN RESPONSE

How can we as Christians effectively share our faith with the Jewish people? First of all, remember the difference between Orthodox, Conservative and Reformed Jews. Second, pray for Israel (Rom 9:2). Third, use the Old Testament Scripture as a basis for dialogue as opposed to focusing on Rabbinical traditions. The authority rests with the Scripture. Finally, focus on Jesus and the fact that the early believers were Orthodox Jews.

May our prayer be that of the Psalmist:

I rejoiced with those who said to me, "Let us go to the house of the Lord." Our feet are standing in your gates, O Jerusalem. Jerusalem is built like a city that is closely compacted together. That is where the tribes go up, the tribes of the Lord, to praise the name of the Lord according to the statute given to Israel. There the thrones for judgment stand, the thrones of the house of David.

Pray for the peace of Jerusalem: "May those who love you be secure. May there be peace within your walls and security within your citadels." For the sake of my brothers and friends, I will say, "Peace be with you." For the sake of the house of the Lord our God, I will seek your prosperity.

PSALM 122

5

Is The East Really Enlightened?

HE IMPACT OF THE EASTERN RELIGIONS, particularly Hinduism and Buddhism, can clearly be seen in New Age philosophy which permeates western culture. Modern New Age beliefs and practices are rooted in these ancient religions and philosophies. As Solomon asked: "Is there anything of which one can say, 'Look! This is something new?' It was here already, long ago; it was here before our time" (Ecc 1:10).

Have you ever noticed how so many modern religious and philosophical systems echo common themes? Bob Larson, in *New Book of Cults*, asks:

Why is it so many cults deny the existence of evil,
the personality of God, and the necessity of an
atoning Savior? Why do they gravitate so often to
reincarnation, astrology, and other occult practices? Why is there such reverence for the *man*
Jesus, but no recognition of his sinless deity? And
why is the Bible quoted so often, but at the same
time denied the importance of its validity? Is there
something or someone behind it all? [11]

Paul gave us insight into the mastermind working
behind the scenes: "The god of this age has blinded the
minds of unbelievers, so that they cannot see the light of
the gospel of the glory of Christ, who is the image of God"
(2 Cor 4:4).

The Eastern religions claim to offer enlightenment to
their followers; an enlightenment which brings peace,
tranquillity and wholeness. The question is, Is the East
really enlightened?

HINDUISM

Hinduism is one of the oldest religions known. Its essence
is stated in the *Vedas*, one of its most sacred writings,
"Truth is one. They call him by different names." Hare
Krishna, Christian Science and other religions derive
many of their beliefs and practices from Hinduism. The
word *Hinduism* is derived from the Sanskrit word Sindhu
or *Indus* (ocean or river). Its chief symbol is the *svastika*

(Sanskrit), called the swastika in the 20th century, meaning, "conducive to well-being." [12]

Mahatma Gandhi once remarked: "A man may not believe in God and still call himself a Hindu." Why does he make such a statement? Because God is regarded as an impersonal force behind the universe linking all elements of creation together as one. All roads eventually lead to God, or enlightenment, including atheism. Hinduism embraces all expressions of religion including pantheism (all is God), monotheism (one God), polytheism (many gods) and atheism (no god). Its all-inclusiveness, however, is its downfall because it keeps the Hindu from God's true revelation of Himself in Jesus Christ.

History

Hinduism began in ancient India from man's desire to know God and to understand the universe. Its primitive religious form, called the *Vedic* religion (from *vedas* meaning knowledge) sought agricultural blessings from the local deities as is characteristic of many primitive religions.

The tribes held to the notion of *animism* which believes that everything in nature possesses a soul or spirit. This belief, in turn, resulted in the worship of everything, including animals. All the spirits were worshipped which formed the essence of the polytheistic religion of the Hindus. They believed that the spirits returned to earth after death in another life form (reincarnation). Since the same life force exists in all elements of creation, whether human or animal, then the spirit could come back in any of these forms. So people may return in another life as animals or insects and vice versa.

Indian history can be divided into four periods. First, the *Pre-Vedic Period* consisted of the earliest settlers in India who were animists.

Secondly the *Vedic Period* (1,500 B.C.) involved the Aryan-Indian conquerors who invaded the area and brought their own gods. The *Vedas* (wise-sayings) were written down about 1,000 B.C. Polytheism developed during this period as well as the caste system consisting of (from highest to lowest): *Brahmins*, priests and teachers; *Kshatriyas*, rulers and soldiers; *Vaishyas*, farmers and merchants; and *Sudras*, peasants and servants. Later on, the caste system was justified on the grounds of karma and reincarnation. Although the caste system is officially outlawed by the Indian government today, it remains alive and well among the Indian villages.

Thirdly, the *Upanishadic Period* (600 B.C.) witnessed a religious shift from the more primitive Vedic beliefs to the philosophical emphasis of the sages. They wrote the 108 poems of the *Upanishads* stressing such concepts as *karma*, *atman* (individual soul), *maya* (illusory nature of matter and reality), *Brahman* (the Universal Soul) and *nirvana* (heavenly state of bliss; the final stage in reincarnation). The two theological pillars of Hinduism include: *polytheism*, the belief that God is one with creation, and *monism*, the concept that "all is one," in the universe.

Finally, the *Vedantic Period* (after Christianity) was characterized by the Vedantic writings being recognized as the primary scriptures. Under the leadership of the philosopher Shankara, who taught that all matter is illusory, including pain and pleasure (*maya*), Hinduism began to focus on self-renuciation and moral duty (*dharma*) as a pathway to freedom and enlightenment as well as inclusion in *nirvana*.

Beliefs and Practices

While many forms of Hindu sacred writings exist, the most supreme are the *Vedas* and the *Upanishads*. The most popular writing is a portion of the Indian epic, *Mahabharata*, called the *Bhagavad-Gita* (the song of the Lord), which emphasizes the importance of transcending desire, pleasure and pain.

Hinduism views God or reality as one essence which takes many forms or expressions (polytheism). The human spirit is divine and longs for union with Brahman (the Universal Soul). This oneness with God eradicates the self. Guilt, sin and the final judgment are illusory concepts so, logically, no concept of atonement or salvation is provided.

There does exist somewhat of a Trinity (although not representative of a personal God) consisting of: *Brahama* the Creator, *Vishnu*, the Preserver, and *Shiva*, the Destroyer. The concept emerged after the dawn of Christianity and probably reflects an attempt to merge the Christian belief in the Trinity into Hinduism. Some 33 million deities exist in Hinduism.

While God is impersonal, the concept of *avatars* developed as a compromise to the belief in a personal God. Avatars are incarnations of deity which appear in each age to help man find his way. The avatars are worshipped as expressions of the divine. The supreme avatar is the god Vishnu who appeared as *Narayana*, as well as Krishna, Rama and others. Partial incarnations of lesser divine forms include *Swamis* (monks), *Sadhus* (holy men who wander around India often naked with cow dung in their hair), and *gurus* (yoga masters).

The purpose of Hinduism is to join the human soul back to the Universal Soul or the Absolute (which can never be described nor defined) from which it came. To do so, four paths to God are offered depending upon the personality of the seeker.

- the *path of devotion* achieved by devotion to a guru is who regarded as an incarnation of the divine;
- the *path of service* characterized by rituals, ceremonies, pilgrimages and good works;
- the *path of knowledge* achieved through the sacred writings and interaction with gurus and sadhus; and
- the *path of contemplation* consisting of meditation and yoga which produces discipline over the mind and body.

While Hinduism gains popularity among some Westerners searching for enlightenment and oneness with the universe, its glaring failure to better the lives of the people in India cannot be ignored. Hinduism fails to deliver what it promises. Furthermore, Hinduism is filled with blatant pagan idolatry including the worship of cows (the mother-goddess of life), rats and other animals as well as an array of ceremonies and rituals. Icons of deities kept in homes are washed, fed, awakened and put to sleep every night as acts of worship (*puja*).

THE CHRISTIAN RESPONSE

The contemporary appeal of Hinduism probably exists in its all-inclusive approach to religions. As opposed to being a well-defined system of belief, it seeks to incorporate into itself all religious beliefs and practices as legitimate paths to God—that is, oneness with the Universal Soul.

The Christian gospel offers lasting answers to the searching questions of Hinduism.

- God, who is personal and can be known through Jesus Christ, answers the mystery of the Unknowable Absolute of Hinduism.
- Resurrection is God's promise which answers the hopeless cycle of reincarnation.
- Grace, which provides forgiveness for the sins of humanity, answers the concept of karma which demands punishment for every evil deed and perfection in life as prerequisites for eternal bliss.
- Jesus, the incarnation of God, answers the myth of the avatars.

BUDDHISM

Buddhism began with an Indian man named Gautama (his family name) Siddhartha (his personal name), born in 563 B.C. near modern day Nepal, India. His name was changed to Guatama Buddha, meaning "enlightened one," after his experience under the famous *Bodhi* (wisdom) tree which brought him enlightenment.

His Experience of Enlightenment

Buddah was born a prince and raised in royal prosperity. He grew up sheltered from the harsh realities of life within the confines of the palace. He married the princess Yasodharma when he was 16. Their son Rahula was born shortly thereafter.

In his early 20's he left the palace to view life outside the security he had known. For the first time in his life he came face to face with suffering. An old man begging. People stricken with disease. A funeral procession. These encounters troubled him deeply. The day he met a Hindu monk changed his life. According to legend the gods incarnated themselves in these images of suffering. He became increasingly dissatisfied with his life of excess. When he was 29 he left the palace, his wife and his son to search for enlightenment which for him meant to experience the peace of nirvana and to understand suffering.

At first he studied under two yoga masters. Then he turned to strict asceticism, subjecting himself to intensely long fasts and to all types of self-afflicted pain. His search ended when he was 35 as he sat under a tree in a forest, where he vowed to stay until he found enlightenment. There he fell into a trance. In the trance he remembered his previous lives.

The legend goes that Mara, the god of death, tried to discourage his efforts to find enlightenment by sending him sensual temptations, which he resisted, followed by life-threatening disasters; but he sat unmoved by the distractions. He reached out his hand and touched the earth which responded with thousands upon thousands of loud roars saying, "I bear you witness."

Suddenly enlightenment came. He was free from all desires and understood all the complex mysteries of life and suffering. Supposedly he remained there for over 40 days in this altered state of consciousness.

His Teachings About Enlightenment
He first shared his experience with five disciples in a nearby deer park. They too experienced enlightenment. For the next 49 years Buddha traveled over India teaching his principles of enlightenment. His teachings constituted, in reality, a reformation within Hinduism; the practices of which he challenged, especially the order of the Brahmin priests for their detachment from common people. He questioned the authority of the Vedic scriptures, and advocated the removal of the caste system and ritual prayers.

As is true of Hinduism in general, Buddha rejected the notions of absolute reality, the concept of God, the existence of good and evil, and the reality of the human soul. His teachings represented something of a middle-of-the-road approach between asceticism and indulgence of desires. He did maintain the Hindu belief in reincarnation and karma. Nirvana, meaning *to blow out*, was defined as a state of bliss in which one is free from all desires.

Buddha taught that suffering results from man's desire for pleasure. The way to end suffering is to extinguish all desires and, thereby, experience nirvana. This is accomplished by following his Eightfold Path to enlightenment:

- *Right Beliefs:* understanding the Four Noble Truths: existence involves suffering (*dukkha*), suffering results from desires for pleasure (*tanha*), extinguishing desire ends suffering, and suffering is ended by following the Eightfold Path.
- *Right Motives:* maintaining pure motives
- *Right Speech:* truthful communication
- *Right Conduct:* Buddha invented his own version of the ten commandments:
    (1) You shall not kill any living creature.
    (2) You shall not take what is not yours.
    (3) You shall not commit adultery.
    (4) You shall not lie, but speak the word of truth.

(5) You shall not partake of
   intoxicating liquors.
(6) You shall not partake of food after
   midday.
(7) You shall not attend any drama,
   dance, or musical performance.
(8) You shall not use any personal
   adornment or perfume.
(9) You shall not sleep on a broad,
   comfortable bed.
(10) You shall not own any gold or
   silver.

- *Right Vocation:* one's work must promote life and harm no one.
- *Right Effort:* determination to follow the Four Noble Truths.
- *Right Thinking:* control of thoughts for self-examination.
- *Right Concentration:* achieved through meditation and raja-yoga.

As an atheist, Buddha placed man at the center of the universe and gave no attention to the origin of humanity. Ignorance, not sin, is the problem of humanity which causes all suffering. Concepts of heaven and hell, as well as a belief about the end of the world, are non-existent in Buddhism. We are to look inward—to discover the Buddha within us all—not upward to God for enlightenment and truth.

Bob Larson points out that while Buddhism appears to be a simple system of belief, in reality it comprises one of the most complex of all Oriental faiths. In addition to the Four Noble Truths and the Eightfold Path, a multiplicity of other practices are required for one to achieve enlightenment including: *Arahatship* (being worthy) consisting of 37 precepts which must be followed devoutly; conquering the five obstacles to enlightenment—sloth, pride, malice, lust and doubt; adhere to 227 regulations including avoiding any touch with a woman (including one's mother) and drinking unstrained water (lest they kill a living thing); man has no soul but exists only in body, emotions, ideas, will and pure consciousness; and nirvana, the state of perfect enlightenment, which is only achieved through successive transmigrations in reincarnated states based on one's karma. Such complete awareness frees one from all feeling, including hate and love. [13]

Buddha died around the age of 80 (480 B.C.). His teachings continued to expand throughout the Orient and to the Mideast, including Israel and Egypt. By the third century A.D. Buddhism had moved into the Far East, and by the sixth and seventh centuries, came to Japan and Tibet. Today Buddhism has been imported by the West, which seems preoccupied with the eastern religions in its search for enlightenment.

Two branches of Buddhism exist: *Mahayana*, consisting of two sub-categories, Pure Land and Zen Buddhism, and

Hinayana. Mahayana is more liberal than Hinayana, believing that all will be saved. It consists of lighter rules and regulations than does Hinayana, which consists primarily of monks and priests, who will be the only ones saved.

Two forms of Buddhism are invading the West, especially America: *Tibetan Buddhism* and *Zen-Buddhism.* *Tibetan Buddhism* originated in A.D. 747 as a blend of sorcery and Buddhism under a pagan exorcist named Padina Sambhava. Practices involve spells, secretive rituals and the use of mantras and mandalas (circular cosmograms of the universe). They developed the concept of *Shambhala,* a kingdom of enlightened ones. *The Book of the Dead* speaks of demons, spirits and powers of witchcraft which must be avoided and appeased.

More recently, in 1951 Communist soldiers invaded the Tibetan kingdom. The Dalai Lama, who was worshipped by his followers as a god-king, fled from the Chinese in 1959 with 110,000 refugees and settled in India. He has toured the West including the United States, and been hailed as a great spiritual leader by some ecumenical religious leaders.

The essence of Tibetan Buddhism is stated by Dalai Lama himself: "If the situation can be fixed, there is nothing to worry about. If it can't be fixed, there is nothing to worry about. After all, things are due to past karma." Tibetan Buddhism continues to gain a foothold in America with its occultic emphases. [14]

Zen-Buddhism is probably the most popular and wide-spread form of Buddhism in the West. The founder of Zen is Bodhidharma, who studied Buddhism in India for 40 years and then returned to China. He sat in a cave for nine years staring at a wall. His legs atrophied and he cut off his eye lids to sustain open-eye meditation.

Zen focuses on *koans*, paradoxical questions such as, "If a tree falls in the woods, and there is no one present to hear it, does it make a sound?" The goal of *koans* is to go beyond logic and reason which are taboo, to experience intuitive truth. Zen denies dualism of any form including good and evil, time and space, present and future. All that exists is what man conceives. Objective reality is an illusion.

While traditional Buddhism offers enlightenment after several reincarnated lives, Zen promises enlightenment (*satori*) to its followers here-and-now. This, of course, is especially appealing to Westerners who live in the fast lane and want everything now. Zen focuses on meditation aimed at emptying the mind of all earthly thoughts. The only comfort used during seated meditation (*zazen*) is a pillow. Any object—a rock, a flower, an idol of Buddha—can be used for meditation.

THE CHRISTIAN RESPONSE

Buddhism is becoming more popular in the United States because it focuses on the self, requires no obedience to a higher authority (God), and defines truth as personal experience, not objective reality. It remains a great tragedy that the spiritual vacuum created in America by secularism is being filled in part by the eastern philosophy.

The Christian gospel offers the Buddhist the joy of knowing God personally and experiencing true revelation from the Holy Spirit. The problem with humanity is not ignorance and the answer is not enlightenment. The problem is sin and the answer is salvation through Jesus Christ.

Buddha gave no attention to the Origin of Humanity.

We do not lack fulfillment, because we are unenlightened; we lack fulfillment because we are separated from God. Jesus is the priest for the world, bridging the gap caused by sin; He alone reconciles us to God. Fulfillment is not found in emptying our minds; it is found when we are filled with the fullness of God. This is why the Bible says that the early disciples were "filled with the Holy Spirit and with joy" (Acts 13:52). Joy comes from the fullness of God.

The East is not really enlightened but remains in the darkness. Enlightenment comes from God who has revealed Himself to us in His Son Jesus Christ. John tells us, "In Him was life, and his life was the light of all men" (Jn 1:4). The enlightenment we all need is a greater understanding of God's love for us and His eternal plan of salvation.

As Paul prayed:

I keep asking that the God of our Lord Jesus Christ, the glorious Father, may give you the Spirit of wisdom and revelation, so that you may know Him better. I pray also that the eyes of your heart may be enlightened in order that you may know the hope to which He has called you, the riches of His glorious inheritance in the saints, and His incomparably great power for us who believe.

EPHESIANS 1:16,17

6

War In The Heavenlies

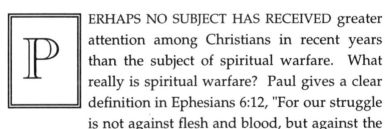

FOR OUR STRUGGLE IS NOT AGAINST
FLESH AND BLOOD.
EPHESIANS 6:12

ERHAPS NO SUBJECT HAS RECEIVED greater attention among Christians in recent years than the subject of spiritual warfare. What really is spiritual warfare? Paul gives a clear definition in Ephesians 6:12, "For our struggle is not against flesh and blood, but against the rulers, against the authorities, against the powers of this dark world and against the spiritual forces of evil in the heavenly realms."

The spiritual war is presented clearly in Scripture. The war began in the Garden of Eden (Gen 3:1-15); is seen in the temptation of Christ (Matt 4:1-11); is addressed by

Christ (Matt 16:18; Luke 10:19; Luke 22:31); and is foremost in the minds of the New Testament writers. Paul tells us to "war a good warfare" (1 Tim 1:18), to "fight the good fight of faith" (1 Tim 6:12), to "endure hardship as a good soldier" (2 Tim 2:3), and to "put on the full armor of God so that you can take your stand against the devil's schemes" (Eph 6:11). The Apostle Peter exhorts us, "Be self-controlled and alert. Your enemy the devil prowls around like a roaring lion looking for someone to devour. Resist him, standing firm in the faith" (1 Peter 5:8,9). James reminds us to "resist the devil and he will flee from you," and John the beloved gives us a word of victory, "Greater is he that is in you than he that is in the world" (1 Jn 4:4).

The critical question is, Who is the enemy and where is the battleground? Understanding the enemy and the battleground on which we fight is crucial to achieving victory.

Victor Hugo said, "A good general must penetrate the brain of his enemy." Field Marshall Montgomery, commander of the allied forces in the North African campaign against Rommel, often quoted the Chinese proverb: "If you know yourself and your adversary clearly, then in a hundred battles you will win a hundred times."

This is exactly what Paul meant when he wrote, "in order that Satan might not outwit us. For we are not ignorant of his schemes" (2 Cor 2:11). The word translated as "schemes" means strategies, tactics, plans, purposes and cunning.

SURVEYING THE BATTLEGROUND

The battleground for the war is located "in the heavenly realms" (Eph 6:12). In his book, *That None Should Perish*, Ed Silvoso states, "In order to take the gospel to every creature, the Church is called to engage the forces of evil. The battleground is the heavenly places. This is where the battle for our cities is won or lost...In order to reach our cities for Christ, the Church must engage and defeat the occupying army of demons under Satan's command who are blinding the lost to the light of the gospel." [15]

The phrase, "in the heavenly realms," appears five times in the book of Ephesians and simply means "the spiritual realm" (1:3; 1:20,21; 2:6; 3:10; 6:10-12). The ancients viewed the heavenlies in three dimensions.

The first heaven consists of the earth's atmosphere. The second heaven consists of the spiritual realm of angels and demons. Angels are mentioned 108 times in the Old Testament and 165 times in the New Testament. The book of Acts records some 20 references to angels being dispatched to the battlefield to assist the Church through times of testing and confusion. In the Old Testament people were forbidden to worship the "great idols" or "demons" (Lev 17:7), and yet we find them sacrificing "their sons and daughters to demons" (Ps 106:37; Deut

32:17). The New Testament provides a thorough profile of evil at work in the spiritual realm with 80 references to *demons,* six to *evil spirits* and 23 to *unclean spirits.*

It is important at this point to review what the Bible teaches about Satan and his method of operation. Satan's diabolical nature is reflected in his titles given in Scripture.

- *Appolyon* (Hebrew), *Abbadon* (Greek): "*destroyer*" (Rev 9:11)
- *Beelzebub*: "*Worthless One*"; *The Prince of Demons* (Matt 9:34; 10:25; 12:24)
- *The Deceiver:* first and last biblical portraits are as a deceiver (1 Tim 2:14; Rev 12:9; Rev 20:8-10)
- *Devil*: "*accuser, slanderer, destroyer, deceiver*" (Rev 12:10; Matt 13:39) The Greek root means "*false witness.*" The term "devil" speaks of him being frightful in appearance, wicked in action, horrible in manner and monstrous in effect.
- *Dragon:* fierceness as our enemy (Rev 12:7)
- *Enemy:* (Matt 13:25, 28, 39; Lk 10:19)
- *Evil One*: fundamental moral attribute; "*wicked one*" (Matt 13:19,38)
- *Father of Lies:* enemy of the truth (Jn 8:44)
- *God of this Age:* (2 Cor 4:4)
- *Murderer From the Beginning*: "man-slayer" (Jn 8:44)

- *Prince*: called the prince of the air, of demons and of this world (Lk 22:53; Jn 16:11; Matt 9:34; Eph 2:2)
- *Satan*: *"adversary, opposing spirit"* used 18 times in Old Testament and 35 times in the New Testament (Zech 13:1; Lk 10:18; Lk 22:31)
- *Serpent*: subtlety and deception (Gen 3:1, Rev 12)
- *Tempter*: (Matt 4:1-11; 1 Tim 2:14)

Satan's strategy is revealed through his imitation of God. Like God, he has:

- *Trinity*: the devil, the beast and the false prophet (Rev 16:13)
- *Church*: "a synagogue of Satan" (Rev 2:9)
- *Ministers*: "ministers of Satan" (2 Cor 11:4-5)
- *System of Theology*: "doctrine of demons" (1 Tim 4:1)
- *Sacrificial System*: "the Gentiles...sacrificed to demons" (1 Cor 10:20)
- *Communion Service*: "the cup of demons...and the table of demons" (1 Cor 10:21)
- *His Own Gospel*: "a gospel contrary to that which we have preached to you" (Gal 1:7-8)
- *Throne*: (Rev 13:2)
- *Worshipers*: (Rev 13:4)
- *A System of Religion*: including false *christs* (Matt 24:4,5), false *teachers* (2 Peter 2:1), false *prophets*

(Matt 24:11), false *brethren* (Gal 2:4) and false *apostles* (2 Cor 11:13).

Satan's work is carried out through what the Bible calls demons.

What are demons? Demons are fallen angels who pledged their allegiance to Satan, the Prince of Demons in opposition to God. Their activity is focused on destroying humanity, the object of God's redeeming love.

What do demons do? Scripture gives different names for demons revealing their work and activity: *familiar spirits* (1 Sam 28:8), *seducing spirits* (1 Tim 4:1), *spirit of divination* (Acts 16:16), *spirit of infirmity* (Luke 13:11), *spirit of prostitution* (Hosea 4:10; 5:4) and the *spirit of falsehood* (1 John 4:6).

Demons operate through a variety of means identified in Scripture.

- *Sorcery* (Acts 13:8, Rev 21:8)
- *Witchcraft* (Ex 22:18; Gal 5:19,20)
- *Astrology* (Deut 18:10-12; Isa 47:13; Dan 2:27; Dan 4:7)
- *Fortune telling* (Dan 4:7; Acts 16:16)
- *Magic arts*, charms or spells (Ex 7:11,12)
- *Necromancy*, contacting the dead (Deut 18:11; Lev 19:31; Isa 19:3)
- *False prophecy* (Matt 7:15)
- *Deceptive signs* (2 Thess 2:9, 10; Rev 16:13-16)

Four levels of demonic activity can be identified:

- *Temptation*: allurement to sin
- *Oppression*: heaviness of spirit; spiritual depression
- *Obsession*: preoccupation with the occult and demonology
- *Possession*: total control and dominance of an individual

As "the prince of the kingdom of the air" (Eph 2:2), Satan tempts humanity to sin through the agency of the world system (*kosmos*, Greek). Thus "the whole world lies in the power of the evil one" (1 John 5:19, NASB) or "the whole world is under the control of the evil one" (NIV).

It is important to differentiate between the *world*, which refers to the attitudes, values, beliefs and lifestyles contrary to God's will (Rom 12:2; 1 Jn 2:15-17) and the *earth*, which belongs to God and is under His watchful care (Ps 24:1; Matt 10:29-31). Satan rules where people follow, "the ways of this world and of the ruler of the kingdom of the air, the spirit who is now at work in those who are disobedient" (Eph 2:3).

There are those who dismiss the reality of satanic activity in human affairs. However, Jesus confirmed His messianic mission by overthrowing demonic forces (Matt 12:22-28). In the New Testament deliverance from demonic power provide a fundamental element in the Church's commission (Matt 10:1; Mk 16:17; Acts 8:7; 16:18).

Two equal errors need to be avoided in the arena of demonology: (1) overstating the role of demons which results in spiritual hysteria, and (2) underestimating the reality of Satan's existence and work. Satanic assaults against the church are real.

As our enemy he perverts the scripture, opposes God's work, hinders the gospel, accuses the brethren, tempts to sin, works lying wonders, appears as an angel of light, brings apostasy to the church and sows discord among the brethren.

Finally, the third heaven speaks of the dwelling of God (2 Cor 12:2). The risen and glorified Christ has passed "through the heavens" (Heb 4:14), and now, having "ascended higher than all the heavens" (Eph 4:10), reigns eternally as "exalted above the heavens" (Heb 7:26).

Spiritual warfare transpires *in the heavenly realms*. The five Ephesian passages, in which Paul speaks of the heavenly realms, provide vital insights for waging war in the supernatural realm.

PRINCIPLE ONE:
The Church Is Blessed In The Heavenlies.

Praise be to the God and Father of our Lord Jesus Christ, who has blessed us in the heavenly realms with every spiritual blessing in Christ (Eph 1:3).

On the basis of Christ's triumphant resurrection and enthronement in the heavenly realms, the purposes and plans of God are worked out in the world. Believers are chosen in Him (1:4), predestined to be His sons (1:5,6), redeemed by His blood (1:7,8), participants in His will (1:9-11), and marked with a seal, the promised Holy Spirit (1:13,14).

Furthermore, Paul tells God's plan of salvation began before the creation of the world (1:4); was based on the sacrifice of Christ (1:5,7); was consummated in the Messianic Kingdom (1:10); will be secured by the sovereignty of God (1:12); and is guaranteed by the deposit of the Spirit in our hearts (1:14).

In this passage Paul destroys any false notion of a dualistic universe that evil is regarded as an equally opposite force to good. God transcends His universe with sovereign power fulfilling His will for humanity in and through the redemptive work of Christ.

In the words of the psalmist, "power belongs to God" (Ps 62:11). Dualism is refuted in Scripture as seen in Satan's description as a *prince*, never as a king. God alone reigns as King (Ps 24:1-10). Satan is called the prince of this world (Jn 12:31), the prince of demons (Matt 9:34; 12:24), the prince of darkness (Lk 22:53), and the prince of the kingdom of the air (Eph 2:2). As a prince he remains under the sovereign, absolute rule of God.

Principle Two:
Christ Reigns Supremely In The Heavenlies.

That power is like the working of His mighty strength,
which He exerted in Christ when He raised Him from the
dead and seated Him at His right hand in the heavenly realms,
far above all rule and authority, power and dominion, and
every title that can be given, not only in the present age
but also in the one to come (Eph 1:19b-21).

Adam and Eve were created to rule over the earth (Gen 1:26,27). However, when Adam sinned he forfeited his rightful authority to rule the earth as God's kingdom representative. As a result he, and all humanity with him, became slaves to sin living under the dominion of Satan (Rom 5:14-17; 6:16). At the Fall Satan became the "god of this world" (2 Cor 4:4).

When Satan tempted Jesus, he offered Him all the kingdoms of this world if Christ would bow down and worship him. Listen to his words, "I will give you all their authority and splendor, for it has been given to me, and I can give it to anyone I want to" (Lk 4:6). It is interesting that Jesus did not challenge Satan's claim to rule over the world's kingdoms.

The question is, Who gave Satan this authority? In response, Adam forfeited his authority when he sinned.

Then came the second Adam—Jesus Christ. He destroyed the curse of sin through His death and resurrection. God's law demanded the death penalty for sin (Rom 3:23; Ezek 18:4) and condemned all people as guilty of sin (Rom 7:9-11). Satan fulfilled the role of the accuser demanding that the sentence of death be carried out (Job 1:6; Zech 3:1; Rev 12:10). However, at Calvary, Christ took upon Himself the sin of the world, received the judgment of God in our place, and secured God's pardon for all humanity (Isa 53:5-6; Rom 3:25,26; 2 Cor 5:18-21).

As a result a kingdom transfer occurs for those who receive Jesus Christ by faith. Paul writes, "For he has rescued us from the dominion of darkness and brought us into the kingdom of the Son he loves" (Col 1:13).

Believers can now answer the accusation of the devil ("slanderer") with a confidence that announces, "Therefore, there is now no condemnation for those who are in Christ Jesus" (Rom 8:1).

Because of Calvary all heaven declares in joyful praise:

Now have come the salvation and the power and the kingdom of our God, and the authority of His Christ. For the accuser of our brothers, who accuses them before God day and night, has been hurled down. They overcame him by the blood of the Lamb and by the word of their testimony; and they did not love their lives so much as to shrink from death (Rev 12:10,11).

The references in Ephesians to Christ being seated far above all rule and authority, power and dominion reiterate Satan's loss of authority over humanity through Jesus' crucifixion, resurrection and ascension. His redemptive work delivered humanity from the slavery of sin, the means by which Satan originally gained dominion.

John the Revelator saw the glorified Christ who declared His victory, "Fear not; I am the first and the last: I am he that liveth and was dead; and behold, I am alive forevermore, amen; and have the keys of hell and of death" (Rev 1:17,18). John assures us of Satan's defeat when he writes, "there were loud voices in heaven, which said: 'The kingdom of the world has become the kingdom of our Lord and of His Christ, and he will reign for ever and ever'" (Rev 11:15).

PRINCIPLE THREE:
The Church Represents Christ's Authority In The Heavenlies.

And God raised us up with Christ and seated us with Him
in the heavenly realms in Christ Jesus (Eph 2:6,7).

Not only does Christ hold the keys of death and hell, He entrusted the keys, symbolic of authority, into the hands of His Body, the Church. Thus Paul says, "And God placed all things under his feet and appointed him to be the head over everything *for the church*, which is his body" (Eph 1:22,23a).

The key phrase is *"for the church."* The resurrected Christ who announced, "All authority in heaven and on earth has been given to me" (Matt 28:18) also declared to His disciples, "Behold, I give you authority" (Luke 10:19) and "I will give you the keys of the kingdom of heaven; whatever you bind on earth will be bound in heaven, and whatever you loose on earth will be loosed in heaven" (Matt 16:18).

Notice that Jesus does not speak of keys *to* the kingdom, but rather the keys *of* the kingdom referring to our representation of His kingdom authority. Furthermore He uses the future tense, "I will give you the keys," a promise fulfilled after His Passion and Resurrection at the outpouring of the Holy Spirit on the Day of Pentecost.

The early believers left the Upper Room "endued with power from on High" (Luke 24:49) ministering the authority of Jesus Christ to people "to open their eyes and turn them from darkness to light, and from the power of Satan to God, so that they may receive forgiveness of sins and a place among those who are sanctified by faith" (Acts 26:18).

The dimension of spiritual authority exercised by the Church in the spiritual realm is expressed in the phrase "in the name of Jesus." The name of Jesus refers to His person, power and presence. In the name (authority) of Jesus the Church gathers for worship (Matt 18:20), baptizes converts (Matt 28:19), preaches the gospel (Lk 24:47), prays in faith (Jn 14:13), delivers those who are demonized (Mark 16:17), and ministers to the sick (Jas 5:14).

Paul reminds us, "And whatever you do, whether in word or deed, do it all in the name of the Lord Jesus, giving thanks to God the Father through Him" (Col 3:17). The name of Jesus speaks of the authority of Jesus which the Church represents and enforces in the spiritual realm.

The delegated authority of Christ to His Church is what Paul has in mind when he reminds us, "We are therefore Christ's ambassadors, as though God were making His appeal through us" (2 Cor 5:20). An *ambassador* (*presbeutes*, Greek) is a messenger and a representative. More specifically the ambassador is one who is:

- *mature*, having the advantage of experience;
- *responsible*, not for his own word but for the word of another whom he serves;
- *commissioned* to bring hostiles into the kingdom or nation he represents;
- *never ashamed* to implore because of the nobility of his calling; and
- *represents another* in his name and authority.

Most importantly the Roman ambassador, which Paul has in mind, spoke with the full authority of the Emperor himself. His primary role was to make sure that rebellion did not erupt in the imperial provinces of Rome. In the same way the Church penetrates a world living in rebellion and hostility to God (Eph 2:1-3) proclaiming the message of Christ with authority, "Be reconciled to God" (2 Cor 5:20).

Behold I give you authority.

The question emerges: In what areas of life does the Church exercise this authority? In response the Church exercises Christ's authority in three primary areas: the balance of power in human affairs (Ps 149:6-9; Matt 5:13-15; 1 Tim 2:1-3); the restraint of evil in the world (2 Thess 2:1-8); and the salvation of the lost (Jn 20:21-23; Rev 22:17).

PRINCIPLE FOUR:
God Displays His Power Through The Church In The Heavenlies.

> *His intent was that now, through the church, the*
> *manifold wisdom of God should be made known*
> *to the rulers and authorities in the heavenly realms,*
> *according to His eternal purpose which He accomplished*
> *in Christ Jesus our Lord (Eph 3:10,11).*

When Adam and Eve sinned, Satan was convinced that humanity was lost forever, hopelessly condemned in its sin. By what means could sinful man ever hope to be reconciled to a holy God? It seemed as though Satan would forever hold humanity as a prisoner to sin.

Yet in Eden, the very place of man's sin, God spoke the first prophecy of Messiah announcing man's deliverance. To the Serpent God declared, "And I will put enmity between you and the woman, and between your offspring and hers; he will crush your head, and you will strike his heel" (Gen 3:15).

The prophecy was fulfilled at Calvary. Satan struck Messiah's heel at the crucifixion but Jesus crushed Satan's head through His resurrection, once and for all liberating humanity from the dominion of darkness.

The crushing of Satan's head refers to his loss of the authority which Adam forfeited in the Fall. Paul declared, "And having disarmed the powers and authorities, he made a public spectacle of them, triumphing over them by the cross" (Col 2:15). Satan has no authority.

The writer of Hebrews tells us, "Since the children have flesh and blood, he too shared in his humanity so that by death he might destroy him who holds the power of death—that is, the devil—and free those who all their lives were held in slavery by their fear of death" (Heb 2:14, 15). As Christ approached the cross He announced, "Now is the time for judgment on this world; now the prince of this world will be driven out" (Jn 12:31).

God's answer to man's estrangement from Him was grace. Only grace could satisfy both the justice of God's law and man's need for mercy. Paul expounds this truth when he writes:

> God presented him (Jesus) as a sacrifice of atonement...to demonstrate his justice, because in his forbearance he had left the sins committed beforehand unpunished—he did it to demonstrate his justice at the present time, so as to be just and the one who justifies those who have faith in Jesus (Rom 3:25,26, parenthesis added).

This is the mystery which Paul said was hidden throughout the ages from the rulers of darkness. "None of the rulers of this age understood it, for if they had, they would not have crucified the Lord of glory" (1 Cor 2:8).

Why does he say this? Because Satan's attempt to kill the Messiah through the crucifixion was the very means through which Satan lost dominion of humanity. When we understand this mystery of grace manifested at the Cross we cannot help but declare with the Apostle Paul, "Oh, the depth of the riches of the wisdom and knowledge of God! (Rom 11:33).

PRINCIPLE FIVE:
The Church Must Exercise Authority In The Heavenlies.

Finally, be strong in the Lord and in his mighty power. Put on the full armor of God so that you can take your stand against the devil's schemes. For our struggle is

not against flesh and blood, but against the rulers,
against the authorities, against the powers of this dark
world and against the spiritual forces of evil
in the heavenly realms (Eph 6:10-12).

Some may logically ask, If Satan has been stripped of his authority, in what sense can we speak of a spiritual war still taking place? In response we must distinguish between *redemption accomplished* and *redemption applied.* The writer of Hebrews tells us plainly that "in putting everything under him, God left nothing that is not subject to him. *Yet at present we do not see everything subject to him.* But we see Jesus, who was made a little lower than the angels, but now crowned with glory and honor" (Heb 2:8,9a, emphasis added).

In other words while Jesus does indeed reign as Lord of all, whose redemption is fully complete, the full appropriation of that redemption is yet to be realized in human history. Until the return of Christ, when Satan will be bound during the millennial kingdom and then ultimately destroyed in the lake of fire (Rev 20:1-15), Satan and the demon spirits under his command will continue to interfere with and influence human affairs.

Thus our conflict is not in the physical/temporal realm but in the unseen/spiritual realm where Christ has seated us as the representatives of His authority in the world.

The role of the Church in the world is a militant one echoed in the call of Jeremiah the prophet: "See, today I appoint you over nations and kingdoms to uproot and tear down, to destroy and overthrow, to build and to plant" (Jer 1:10). Christ Himself spoke of His Church in terms of conquest, "Upon this rock I will build my church and the gates of hell (literally, "powers of death") shall not prevail against it" (Matt 16:18, parenthesis added).

Since the battleground is the heavenlies and the enemy is neither flesh or blood, our weaponry is also spiritual in nature. Paul writes, "For though we live in the world, we do not wage war as the world does. The weapons we fight with are not the weapons of the world. On the contrary, they have divine power to demolish strongholds" (2 Cor 10:3,4).

While a thorough list of weaponry is provided in Paul's description of the armor of God, (Eph 6:11-17), including the belt of truth, the breastplate of righteousness, the shoes of peace, the shield of faith, the helmet of salvation and the sword of the Spirit, the one weapon which empowers every other weapon is the weapon of intercessory prayer.

He completes the list of offensive and defensive weaponry by urging us to "pray in the Spirit on all occasions with all kinds of prayers and requests. With this in mind, be alert and always keep on praying for all the saints" (Eph 6:18). Prayer restrains the work of demonic forces and releases the power of God.

Daniel, the prophet, learned this principle during his 21-day fast. At the end of his fast, an angel touched him, strengthened him, and said to him, "Since the first day...

your words were heard, and I have come in response to them. But the prince of the Persian Empire resisted me 21 days" (Dan 10:12-13a).

The angel goes on to tell Daniel that the archangel Michael assisted him in the battle in the heavenlies. The passage underscores the reality of demonic forces as they influence political kingdoms and rule over geographical areas. It also connects the principle of prevailing prayer with war in the heavenlies.

Prayer is where the action is. John Wesley noted that "God will do nothing apart from the prayers of His people." E.M. Bounds said, "every Christian who ever did anything for the Lord was characterized by that notable quality called prayer." Paul E. Billheimer, in the book, *Destined For the Throne*, makes the challenge that "any Church without a well-organized and systematic prayer program is simply treading a religious treadmill." [16]

Billheimer's insights regarding warfare prayer are thought-provoking:

> Prayer is not begging God to do something which He is loath to do. It is not overcoming reluctance in God. It is enforcing Christ's victory over Satan. It is implementing upon earth Heaven's decisions concerning the affairs of men. Calvary legally destroyed Satan, and canceled all of his claims. God placed the enforcement of Calvary's victory in the hand of the Church (Matt 18:18 and Luke 10:17-19). He has given her "power of attorney."

She is His "deputy." But this delegated authority is wholly inoperative apart from the prayers of a believing Church. Therefore, prayer is where the action is. [17]

Silvoso agrees with Billheimer's challenge by writing, "The believer is a deputy of the Court of Calvary assigned to enforce the judgment awarded to Jesus: the salvation of the lost. The believer is to use this

Pray in the spirit.

delegated authority mainly in prayer." [18] The statement is true—"The fate of the world is in the hands of nameless saints"—saints who dare to war in the heavenlies through the power of intercessory prayer.

Perhaps the Psalmist expressed it best:

> *May the praise of God be in their mouths*
> > *and a double-edged sword in their hands,*
> *to inflict vengeance on the nations*
> > *and punishment on the peoples,*
> *to bind their kings with fetters,*
> > *their nobles with shackles of iron,*
> *to carry out the sentence written against them.*
> > *This is the glory of all his saints. Praise the Lord.*
> > > PSALM 149:5-9

NOTES

CHAPTER ONE: THE MAIN BUSINESS

1. George Barna, *Evangelism That Works*, (Dallas: Word Publishing, 1992), p. 31.
2. *The Pastor's Weekly Briefing*. Vol. 3, No. 29, July, 1995.

CHAPTER TWO: THE INVASION OF ISLAM

3. Sai'd Al-Ashmawy, "Islam's Real Agenda," *Reader's Digest*, January, 1996, p. 157.
4. Ibid, p. 159.

CHAPTER THREE: WHAT'S NEW ABOUT NEW AGE?

5. Robert Lindsey, "Spiritual Concepts Drawing a Different Breed of Adherent," *New York Times*, September 29, 1986.
6. Fergus M. Bordewich, "Colorado's Thriving Cults," *New York Times Magazine*, May, 1988, pp. 37-42.
7. Daniel L. Black, "The Familiar and Deceptive Language of the New Agers," *Evangel Magazine*, October, 1992, p. 7.
8. Sharon Beekmann, "Deliver Us From Evil," *Moody Monthly*, March/April, 1996, p. 96.

CHAPTER FOUR: JUDAISM AND JESUS

9. Walter Elwell, Editor, *Evangelical Dictionary of Theology*, (Grand Rapids: Baker Books, 1984), pp. 589-590.

10. William Barclay, *Jesus As They Saw Him*, (Grand Rapids: Eerdmann Publishers, 1962), pp. 111-152.

CHAPTER FIVE: IS THE EAST REALLY ENLIGHTENED?

11. Bob Larson, *New Handbook of Cults*, (Wheaton: Tyndall House, 1982), p. 70.
12. Ibid.
13. Ibid, p. 75.
14. Ibid, p. 77-78.

CHAPTER SIX: WAR IN THE HEAVENLIES

15. Ed Silvoso, *That None Should Perish*, (Ventura: Regal Books, 1994), pp. 97-98.
16. Paul E. Billheimer, *Destined For the Throne*, (Fort Washington: Bethany House, 1975), p. 18.
17. Ibid, p.17.
18. Ed Silvoso, *TNSP*, p. 177.